It's Time for a Praise Break!

by

Dr. Pat McKinstry

Vincom Publishing Co.
Tulsa, Oklahoma

It's Time for a Praise Break!
ISBN 0-927936-32-1
Copyright © 1998 by
Dr. Pat McKinstry
3611 Upton Avenue
Toledo, Ohio 43613

Published by
Vincom Publishing Co.
P. O. Box 702400
Tulsa, Oklahoma 74170
(918) 254-1276

Contents

Dedication

Dedicated to my husband and friend, Luther C. McKinstry Jr., son, Luther C. McKinstry III, and in loving memory of my mother, Lillie M. Scott.

This book is also dedicated to the intercessors who carried this ministry in prayer, fasting and praise. They are now in the presence of the Lord. Principles from the book were taught to them and putting them into practice added many years to their lives, when some of them were given only months to live.

Mother Clara Moore
Elaine Adkins
Rosemary Ambrose
William Sullivan
Cheryl Toler
Elsie Schmitt
Mother Margaret Rudledge
Betty Woolley

Foreword

Having been afforded the privilege of serving in the capacity of Minister of Music for churches ranging in size from 100 to 14,000 over the past twenty years, and of traveling extensively across America as well as in England, Jamaica, South America, Germany, Portugal and Korea, ministering in workshops, seminars and conferences, praise has had a central place and focus in my personal life and ministry.

In many communities during those early years, I often heard, "This is the first praise and worship seminar we have had in this area." During those early years, there was no Hosanna Integrity, and most of the music ministry experience in our churches was void of revelatory substance. It was during this same time period that Phil Driscoll was introduced to me when he had only been saved for ten days. Needless to say, great progress has been realized in the Body of Christ since that time in both the understanding and practice of praise and worship.

In her book, *It's Time for a Praise Break!* Dr. Pat McKinstry teaches scriptural truths about praise and worship that are often overlooked. For example:

• Praise and worship will usher you into the presence of the Lord. In His presence, there is fulness of joy. There is healing. There is comfort. There is peace and assurance.

• When we are overwhelmed, we must learn to go to the Rock Who is higher than we are and take a "praise break."

- We must praise God until an exchange takes place: His strength for our weakness; His love for our lack of it; His peace for our confusion, turmoil and restlessness; and His joy for our heaviness.

Dr. McKinstry encourages the reader to make praise a part of their lifestyle, designating a specific period of time each day where they do nothing but praise the Lord.

Too often we confront one another and try to solve a problem, meet a need, or embark upon an endeavor without taking ample time to first praise the Lord...to allow the realization of the consciousness of Who God is and what He has already done for us through Jesus' completed work at Calvary, to get into our hearts and minds.

As you read *It's Time for a Praise Break!* you will learn the importance of praising the Lord instead of giving up; praising instead of fainting; praising instead of being fearful; praising instead of allowing weakness or symptoms of illness to remain in your body; praising Him instead of entertaining oppressive thoughts.

Dr. Pat McKinstry is a woman of God who has received the revelation of the power of praise from God. May the revelation she shares in this book inspire you, the reader, to pause, call for a time out, and take a "praise break"!

Doyle Tucker, Psalmist

Introduction

One of the attributes of God is that He **is a man of war** (Exodus 15:3). Most people know Him as a man of Peace, a Deliverer, a Healer, a Provider, a Protector — but He is also a Man of war.

The same principle of faith that is used to receive salvation, healing, provision, or anything else from the Lord, is the key to seeing God and His forces rise up supernaturally in our behalf and throw our present-day enemies — the devil and his demons — into the sea. In other words, to stop their attack and assignment against us. That principle of faith is found in 2 Corinthians 4:13:

> **We having the same spirit of faith, according as it is written, I believed, and therefore have I spoken; we also *believe*, and therefore *speak*.**

In this book, I encourage you to stir up the Man of war by *believing* God's Word and *speaking* it in the face of the enemy's attacks through the medium of praise and worship. I call it, *taking a praise break*.

I have given you examples of taking a praise break. Now it's time for you to lift up your voice, both individually and corporately, and offer your praise and worship unto the Lord. As it becomes a part of your lifestyle, you will move to a higher level in your spiritual growth and you will see the enemy of your soul subdued again and again by the Man of war!

Dr. Pat McKinstry

1

Stirring Up the Man of War

The setting of Exodus, chapter 15, comes right after Moses and the children of Israel saw the Egyptians (their enemies) — their horses and riders — thrown into the Red Sea and drowned. The Word of God says there was a force that literally knocked them off their horses into the water.

Verse 1 gives a portion of the song of triumph that Moses and the children began to sing:

> **I will sing unto the Lord, for he hath triumphed gloriously: the horse and his rider** *hath he thrown into the sea.*

Imagine bodies and horses flying around in the Red Sea! That's what happened when God overthrew Pharaoh's army that was going after the Israelites. There are some things getting ready to be thrown for us in a similar supernatural manner!

Verse 2 says:

> **The Lord is my strength and song, and he is become my salvation: he is my God, and I will prepare him an habitation.**

"My strength, my song and my salvation" mean deliverance in every area of life. For God to become all of this, there must be a place prepared where He can dwell or inhabit.

> **My father's God, and I will exalt him.**
>
> *The Lord is a man of war:* **the Lord is his name.**

> **Verses 2,3**

1

Most of us have been taught that God is a God of peace — the Prince of Peace. We need to know the full attributes of the God we worship because He is a Peacemaker and a Giver, but the Word says He is also *a Man of war.*

God can only move in our behalf according to our faith, knowledge and revelation of Him. If we only know Him to be a God Who saves, that's all He will be to us. If we have only been taught that He can save us from our sins, then that's all we are going to know about God. The Word of God wants us to get to know Him as a God Who will be whatever we need Him to be. I AM THAT I AM steps in here!

I not only want to know Him as the God Who heals, saves and supplies my needs, but there are some situations I need Him to get me out of or to deliver me from. We can get into some situations where we need a fighter to go in, defeat our foes, and carry us out. We need to know that God is a God Who will fight for us. This is why we need to know what it is that stirs up the fight in God, what gets Him to stand up off of His throne and what gets Him to move. We need to prepare our habitation for God.

When our praises go up, God's blessings come down. Our praises stir the heart of God to become a Man of war. What is the habitation we need to build for God to become a God of war?

Psalm 22:3 says, **But thou art holy, O thou that inhabitest the praises of Israel** [the praises of His people]. Exodus 15:2 says, **I will prepare him an habitation.** God needs a place to inhabit to become our strength, our peace and our joy. He needs a place where He can dwell so He can become our God of war. Psalm 22:3 says that He inhabits our praises.

The Lord on high is mightier than the noise of many waters (Psalm 93:4).

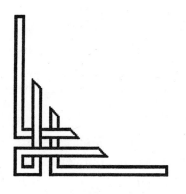

We are going to have to build a place where God can dwell, and *He dwells in our praises*. This let's us know that He doesn't dwell in our murmuring and complaining. That's why we've got to change the way we talk. He doesn't dwell in our crying or self-pity. If we want God to come where we are and become a part of us, that means we've got to have a place of praise. It doesn't happen in church, because we are not in church twenty-four hours a day, seven days a week. This means that praise must become a part of our daily lifestyle.

God dwells where there is praise. Our praises absolutely do something for God. Wherever God dwells means we have His presence. Psalm 16:11 says, **Thou will shew me the path of life: in thy presence is fulness of joy....** What else happens in God's presence? Psalm 68:2 says, **Let the wicked perish at the presence of God.**

So where is God's presence? It is in you and me. That's why we can go into negative circumstances, situations and environments and not even lift our voice or say anything, and God brings in healing, deliverance and peace. If you are a praiser and God dwells within you, then the wicked things must stop when you show up! **The wicked perish at the presence of God.**

The habitation for God to dwell in must be built before you go to your job. You can't go on the assembly line and say, "Hallelujah, praise You, Jesus, or Wonderful Savior," or you could be fired. But if you will build that habitation of praise before you go on your job, you'll see the attitude of your supervisor change, the attitude of your co-workers change. They won't even understand why they hated you at first, but the Spirit of God in you will draw them to you.

Recently, a young woman brought me a praise report. Everything seemed to be against her on her job, but her supervisor called her at home and said, "I don't even know why I've been acting up against you. I have no reason, but I want you to know I'm sorry." While she was praising God, standing in the presence of God, the wicked part of her supervisor had to come down.

When praise becomes a part of your daily lifestyle, God will change people's attitudes and dispositions, because the wicked perish at the presence of God.

I'm not saying that we're going to pass every test, and I'm not telling you that I pass every test. I do not have a halo or wings! We still go to war, and sometimes we feel like we've got to give people a piece of our mind. But if we keep giving out a lot of pieces, we'll have no mind left!

Now, God is giving us revelation knowledge of how to believe and stand on His Word in the midst of adverse circumstances, realizing that we can come to a rest because the battle is not ours but His. How can the battle not be ours when we're in it? That's why God is teaching us that praise wins a lot of battles and that "a piece of our mind" [our words] may add fuel to the fire rather than put it out.

Psalm 9:1-3 says:

I will praise thee, O Lord, with my whole heart; I will shew forth all thy marvellous works.

I will be glad and rejoice in thee: I will sing praise to thy name, O thou most High.

When mine enemies are turned back, they shall fall and perish at thy presence.

The Lord reigneth

(Psalm 97:1).

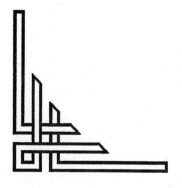

So how do we cause the enemy to back off? By praising the Lord with a whole heart, rejoicing in Him, and singing praise to His name. That's how we get the enemy off our back. God causes His people to triumph as they celebrate Jesus.

The more I encounter circumstances and problems, the more I'm going to praise God, because I have found that praise stirs God up. When I'm into a situation and I don't know how I'm going to get out, as I begin to be glad and rejoice, God causes my enemies to fall and perish at my side.

Let's look at Isaiah 42:10-13:

> *Sing unto the Lord a new song*, **and his praise from the end of the earth, ye that go down to the sea, and all that is therein; the isles, and the inhabitants thereof.**
>
> **Let the wilderness and the cities thereof lift up their voice, the villages that Kedar doth inhabit: let the inhabitants of the rock sing, let them shout from the top of the mountains.**
>
> **Verses 10,11**

Not only do you sing a new song and praise the Lord, but it says to lift up your voice.

> **Let them give glory unto the Lord, and declare his praise in the islands.**
>
> **Verse 12**

When you sing a new song, you praise Him, you raise your voice, you rejoice, you sing for joy, you shout, you give glory and you proclaim His praise, look what happens.

> **The Lord shall go forth as a mighty man, he shall stir up jealousy like a man of war: he shall cry, yea, roar;** *he shall prevail against his enemies.*
>
> **Verse 13**

When we are singing, raising our voices, rejoicing and giving God praise, when we are shouting and making a noise unto
God, we are stirring Him up. Anything that gets in the way of
our giving Him that type of praise — anything that comes to
bewilder us or make us weary or discouraged — stirs up an
anger in God, because He likes us to sing praises, to rejoice,
shout and make a noise before Him. Our praises stir God up,
and as a result, He gives a war cry.

As I was reading in the Word how our praise stirs God up,
I thought of Tarzan. I believe when we start praising God, He
says, "Ahhhaaaahhhhaaa" and He begins to buffet our enemies.
We need to get a good picture of this. Do you think I'm going
to be dignified when I need somebody to fight for me? No! I'm
going to open my mouth and shout unto the Lord. I'm going to
praise God with a praise. I'm going to rejoice in Him so He can
say, "Ahhhaaaahhhhaaa...boom!"

I'm not going to approach God with a "small" voice. That's
why He hasn't moved for some of you. He can't hear you!

God is saying, "When I can find the people who will rejoice
and sing a new song, be joyous in Me and shout My praises, I'm
going to be stirred up to fight for them." That's why He said the
battle is not ours. When we praise God, He says, "I'll fix your
enemies." When we sing praises unto the Lord, we cause Him
to raise the battle cry and triumph over our enemies. We stir up
a zeal in God.

Isn't it amazing that people can go to ball games and shout,
celebrate with their families and make a whole lot of noise, but
when they get in church, they say, "It's just a little bit too loud!"
I've got news for you! I found out in the Word that the louder
we get, the more we stir up God. If you've got a nervous condition, then ask for a transfer, because I need some victory in
my land. It's time to possess the land the Lord has given us.

I will praise thee, O Lord
my God, with all my
heart
(Psalm 86:12).

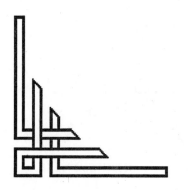

In my church we've had to grow up in learning how to praise the Lord and the importance of it, but there's a whole lot more growing up we need to do. We're not going to be out of order, but we're going to get a holy reverence in this house until we know when to shout and when to worship. We're going to get in some "hallelujahs" and "thank You, Jesus."

I'm not after a popularity contest and I'm not trying to build membership. But I am trying to get a group of people who will get a relationship with God and possess their land.

Psalm 47:1 says, **O clap your hands, all ye people; shout unto God with the voice of triumph.** Shout! I had to ask God to teach me wisdom, as a leader, how to walk in His Word. Sometimes we try to get sophisticated in our praise and worship. I'm telling you right now, I'm not going to get sophisticated for anybody when I need some triumph in my life. No, I'm not! I've got some family members who need to be saved and some things that need to turn for me. I found out that God will go after my enemy. You think I'm going to say a little hallelujah? No!

Every time I open my mouth, I'm calling in my finances. Every time I open my mouth in praise, I turn God on the enemy that is holding my family in captivity. You think I'm going to be quiet? This shouting and making noise is no cultural thing either. There is no culture in heaven. I thank God we're not hung up on culture. There is no black or white, Asian or Hispanic thing.

The Apostle John wrote:

> **I beheld, and, lo, a great multitude, which no man could number, of all nations, and kindreds, and people, and tongues, stood before the throne, and before the Lamb, clothed with white robes, and palms in their hands;** *and cried with a loud voice....*

Revelation 7:9,10

You may be thinking, "By nature I am quiet." That's why you need to be delivered. **If any man be in Christ, he is a new creature...** (2 Corinthians 5:17). Come off of this nature stuff! That's why the devil has been running over your head. "My nature."

If you have some family members who need deliverance, you'd better open your mouth and shout it unto God. Whatever the Word says, we are going to do it. If I've ever been a fool, I'm going to be a fool for God. If He says to shout, I'm going to shout. If He says to worship, I'm going to worship. If He says to laugh, I'm going to laugh. I'm going to do it all because I am going to possess my land. If you are going to possess your land, shout unto God with a voice of triumph.

Psalm 47:5 says, **God is gone up with a shout, the Lord with the sound of a trumpet.** "Gone up" means God is stirred up. He will arise in the midst of a shout. God is stirred up with a shout. I cannot blow a trumpet, but the Word says I can lift my mouth up like a trumpet. I'm going to open my mouth and make a sound like a trumpet. Every time I think about the greatness of God, I blow the trumpet in Zion! God is stirred up at the sound of a trumpet.

Isaiah 30:32 says:

> **And in every place where the grounded staff shall pass, which the Lord shall lay upon him, it shall be with tabrets and harps: and in battles of shaking will he fight with it.**

That means every stroke the Lord lays on the enemy with his punishing rod shall be with music of tambourines and harps. How much of a whooping the devil gets depends on the loudness, the length and the fullness of your praise.

Every stroke that is laid on the enemy with God's punishing rod is going to depend on the tambourines, the music and the praise. So if you want the devil to get a little bit of a beating, just give two little hallelujahs. But if you want him to get whipped and good, hang out and praise for a while!

When my son as growing up, he never liked for me to whip him. I was swinging at him one day when he was about nineteen years old. He was learning how to duck. I aimed at his head and he ducked. I hit my hand on the door and broke two fingers. I couldn't hit him any more because I was in great pain. As I screamed, I yelled for my husband to come. He came running but he didn't know what happened. I said, "Whoop him!" He said, "What for?" I said, "Don't ask me any questions, just whoop him." He said, "Pat, tell me." I said, "Whoop him, we'll talk later."

My husband said, "Come here, June Bug. Your mama told me that I'm supposed to whoop you. I don't know for what, but here it is!"

I said to my husband, "Let's go for a ride." When my son was growing up, we didn't fight or debate in front of him. But we had some strong conversations out of his presence!

God is saying, "I'm going to lay the strokes on the enemy by the sound of worship I hear." If you are calm and unexcited, the stroke will be light. But if you shout, "God, I praise You," He lets the enemy have it. Strokes are laid on him according to the music of the tambourines and harps. This is why I want the musicians to be anointed and to stay anointed. They will help to run the devil off of your back.

God designed music. He designed tambourines. If you've got a little rhythm in your wrist, go and buy you a tambourine.

Psalm 68:1 says, **Let God arise, let his enemies be scattered.** How do we get God to arise? Praise Him! We've got to praise God to stir Him up. If you need some enemies to be scattered, praise God! The word *scattered* means "broken or dashed to pieces." When we stir up God with our praises, we call God to throw our enemies around. That's why Pharaoh's horses and the riders were thrown into the Red Sea. God showed them what praise and worship can do.

Let God arise. Stir God up. Get Him to rise up from His throne and start throwing your enemies off your back. Let God arise. Your enemies will never be scattered if you don't stir Him up. You can only stir Him up with your praise and with your shout, with your singing and with your rejoicing, with you raising your voice, with you giving Him glory and with you proclaiming His praise. That's how you stir God up. Let God arise! Let God arise! Let God arise!

I saw God arise in the hospital. That's why I left it in God's hands and flew off for a two-day vacation when they were running tubes in my father and told me that he had another stroke. They didn't know how bad it was. He wasn't walking or moving and they thought he was paralyzed completely.

Sometimes we operate differently when it begins to strike home, but as I stood there, he couldn't talk, and all of the things that were going on, all I knew was to let God arise. As I walked from the room and walked outside of the hospital, I began to give God praise. I told God, "I can't handle it. I don't know if You are ready to take him. I don't know if he's ready to go, but I know in whom I believe. So regardless of how it works out, God, You are going to condition me for this circumstance."

I decided to let God arise. The enemy said, "You know, you're not going to be there when he passes." I want you to know, they took all the tubes out, and my father is talking and he's up walking.

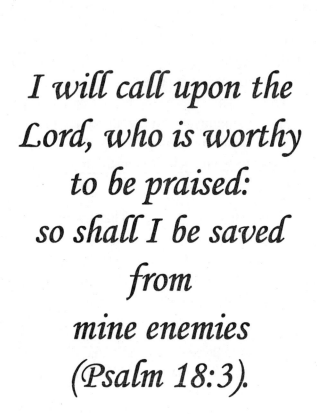

*I will call upon the
Lord, who is worthy
to be praised:
so shall I be saved
from
mine enemies
(Psalm 18:3).*

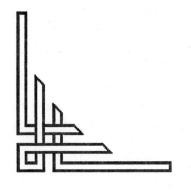

When you let God arise, if He doesn't change it, He will fix you in it. You will be able to praise God in the midst of what is going on. Let God arise!

An Example of High Praise

I always thought I was a praiser. In the forty years I've experienced, I thought I had seen people praise God in everything. But there was one thing that happened in my life, one event that I witnessed, that excelled all praise I had ever witnessed. That was the day I walked into the hospital with Jackie Johnson.

Now, I had told my assistant pastor, "I'm ready to quit being a pastor. I don't want to be a pastor anymore. I can't go on. My heart can't take it." I was at the lowest point I've ever been, having gone through the death of my son and my mother. I said, "I can't take this."

We walked in that room and Jackie picked up her baby, sat in a rocking chair, no breath in its three-year-old body because he was in the presence of the Lord. She sat in the rocking chair and began to sing, "We are more than conquerors, overcomers in this life. We've been made victorious, by the blood of Jesus Christ."

Jackie looked at me and said, "Pastor, come on, help me sing because you taught me how to praise Him." I couldn't sing. She said, "Yes, you can. We are more than conquerors." This was her lifeless baby, and she was imparting strength to me. She kept on singing.

Can you imagine a mother with her dead child, her only child, in her arms? We didn't understand and we still don't understand, but she trusted God in spite of it. She wasn't thanking Him *for* it, but she was praising Him *in the midst of it*! She was able to praise God, and the sound of her praise went all over that hospital. In the Intensive Care Unit where the baby was, the nurses were falling out under God's power. They were carrying ward clerks and doctors off of the floor. What was going on? The anointing of God filled that hospital floor.

We are talking about high praises, when her faith went beyond her emotions. She could have been mad, she could have quit God, she could have said, "God, why did You do it?" But she kept saying, "Hallelujah!" Every time she embraced her baby, she sang, "Hallelujah!" Yet I know her heart was broken.

There are families in our church today who were saved through the praises offered up at that baby's homegoing celebration.

No matter what is going on, we can praise God.

A Scriptural Demonstration of Praise

In Matthew, chapter 21, we see an open demonstration of praise to Jesus as He came riding on a colt. Verses 8 and 9 say:

> **And a very great multitude spread their garments in the way; others cut down branches from the trees, and strawed them in the way.**
>
> **And the multitudes that went before, and that followed, cried, saying, Hosanna to the son of David: Blessed is he that cometh in the name of the Lord; Hosanna in the highest.**

Verse 10 says, **All the city was moved.** But not only was the city moved, Jesus got moved, because the Word says that when Jesus went into the temple, He took a whip and began to chase the enemies out of His Father's house.

> **And Jesus went into the temple of God, and cast out all them that sold and bought in the temple, and overthrew the tables of the moneychangers, and the seats of them that sold doves,**

And said unto them, It is written, *My house shall be called the house of prayer*; but ye have made it a den of thieves.

This wasn't the first time Jesus saw the moneychangers in the temple. He went to the temple all the time, and the same folks were still doing the same things in the temple. Do you know what stirred up the indignation in Christ? It was the praise. The people said, **Blessed is he that cometh in the name of the Lord.** They called the war out of Him! **Hosanna to the son of David** stirred up the zeal in Jesus, so when He got to His Father's house, He knew things were out of order. The praise He heard coming down the road caused Him to take a whip and drive the moneychangers out of the temple. He said, **My house shall be called the house of prayer** (v. 13).

Praise from your own mouth will drive a lot of wrong things out of you. I'm not worried about your habits, drugs, alcohol, or sex life. But I am concerned about you praising and worshipping the Lord, because praise and worship will drive those things out of you. Every time you praise the Lamb Who sits on the throne, He is going to drive everything out of you that shouldn't be there.

Proverbs 27:21 says, **As the fining pot for silver, and the furnace for gold; so is a man to his praise.**

Praise will upset religious systems and make religious people mad. Have you ever heard some of the religious people say, "In the church I come from, we praise God, but we don't have to go through all this because God's not hard of hearing. They just act unseemly. The pastor, too, and they are flying these rags around in the air! They're dancing like the world. It's just a bunch of junk"?

*Great is the Lord,
and
greatly to be praised
(Psalm 48:1).*

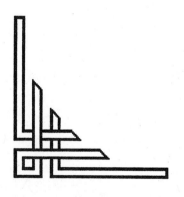

There is no place in the Word that says you're supposed to throw your coat down when you are praising the Lord. There is no place in the Word where it says to cut down branches and throw them before the King. But neither is there Scripture that says you can't do it. You can be demonstrative in praising God.

If I feel like waving a banner up in the air, I'm going to do it. If I feel like walking back and forth, if you can do it for the world, why can't we jam for God? If you can jump up for your favorite ball team, throwing pop corn and pop on yourself, why can't we shout for Jesus? Religious folks can keep their dry religion and dead traditions, but the Word of God says, **If these should hold their peace, the stones would immediately cry out** (Luke 19:40). No stone is going to take my place in praising and worshipping the Lord!

2
Putting the High Praises
in Your Mouth

Praise ye the Lord. Sing unto the Lord a new song, and his praise in the congregation of saints.

Let Israel rejoice in him that made him: let the children of Zion be joyful in their King.

Let them praise his name in the dance: let them sing praises unto him with the timbrel and harp.

For the Lord taketh pleasure in his people: he will beautify the meek with salvation.

Let the saints be joyful in glory: let them sing aloud upon their beds.

Psalm 149:1-5

The song of the Lord is going to get in your belly and in your innermost being, in your bones, in your joints and in your marrow! It's going to become like a fire shut up in your bones. You're going to try to go to sleep, and instead, you will sing a new song unto the Lord.

Let the high praises of God be in their mouth, and a two-edged sword in their hand.

Psalm 149:6

The high praises of God refer to letting go of your emotions, your circumstances and your problems. It means, take a step of faith and when it leads your feelings, your mind and what's going on with you, it becomes a high praise to God. No matter what's going on or what you're facing, if you can get past your problems and what your mind is telling you, it becomes a high praise.

That high praise means a praise of faith: "I don't understand what's going on, but I'm still going to praise the Lord because He is worthy and He is still God."

He said to put that kind of praise in your mouth instead of saying, "God, I don't understand what's going on. I just don't know how I'm going to make it. I've been trying to live right." He says, "Put some high praises in your mouth."

"I just got a bad phone call, but God is still God. A family member just died, but God is still God. My job just shut down, but God is still God. There's trouble in my marriage, but God is still God." Put those high praises in your mouth and a two-edged sword in your hand. Praise God for what His Word says about Him. The Word says, **I am the Lord that healeth thee** (Exodus 15:26). "Thank You, Lord, that You are my Healer."

The two-edged sword says, **The Lord is my shepherd; I shall not want** (Psalm 23:1). "Thank You, Lord, that because You are my Shepherd, I have no lack. I do not want. You will supply all of my need according to Your riches in glory by Christ Jesus (Philippians 4:19). Thank You, Lord, for being my Provider."

The two-edged sword says, **When he, the Spirit of truth, is come, he will guide you into all truth** (John 16:13). "Thank You, Jesus, for Your guidance in my life through the Holy Spirit."

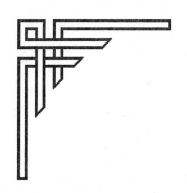

*O Lord our Lord,
how excellent
is thy name in
all the earth!
(Psalm 8:1).*

The two-edged sword says, **Fret not thyself because of evildoers, neither be thou envious against the workers of iniquity...Trust in the Lord, and do good** (Psalm 37:1,3). "Thank You, Lord, that You always cause me to triumph." Continue to put the two-edged sword (the Word) in your heart and the high praises in your mouth.

Verse 7 of Psalm, chapter 149, continues, **To execute vengeance upon the heathen, and punishments upon the people.** It's time for us to execute vengeance upon the heathen. When we look at the word *heathen,* we think it refers to real bad people, but *heathen* means people who don't know God.

To execute or heap vengeance upon the heathen means that our praises will bring an unbeliever under conviction. An unbeliever can't walk into a praise service in an atmosphere of praise and leave the same. (Neither can a believer!) The heathen may be "having a party," but it's only for a season. Hebrews 11:25 says that the pleasures of sin are only for a season.

> **To bind their kings with chains, and their nobles with fetters of iron;**
>
> **To execute upon them the judgment written: this honour have all his saints. Praise ye the Lord.**
>
> **Psalm 149:8,9**

In other words, it's time to put the devil into bondage. We are going to take his weapons and his strength from him. We're going to stop the devil in his tracks with our high praises. We execute vengeance upon the heathen when we tell God that He is holy and that He is our provision. When the devil tells you that you can't make it, come against him with praise, saying, "The Lord is my Shepherd, I shall not want "

When the devil tells you he's going to kill you with a disease, put judgment upon him by worshipping the Lord Who heals you. When the devil tries to tell you that your family will never be saved and delivered, run him off by worshipping the Lord God Almighty with, "Because I believe on You, Lord, both me and my household shall be saved (Acts 16:31)." That's the Word of the Lord. Just have a praise revival in your own heart and life.

Set aside times just to praise the Lord, not asking Him for anything, but just praising Him. Dance before the Lord and thank Him that your family is saved and delivered. Even if you don't know where a family member is, praise the Lord for their salvation. Don't shed another tear, plead another plea, or give another supplication, but praise Him. Instead of crying out for God to help you, take a praise break and thank Him, praise Him and worship Him

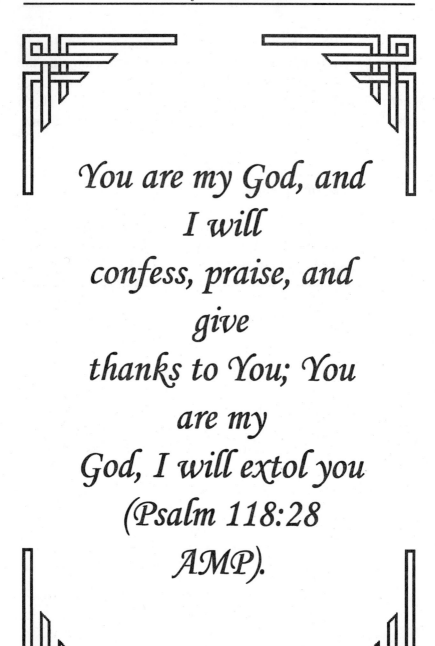

You are my God, and I will confess, praise, and give thanks to You; You are my God, I will extol you (Psalm 118:28 AMP).

3
So What's a "Praise Break"?

Praise is the highest expression of faith. That means it even supersedes prayer. Praise will cause you to break through the second heaven where all the demonic principalities and powers rule and move you into the third heaven in the very presence of God. Your praise will act like UPS or Federal Express! The delivery of what you need will come overnight as you simply praise Him!

Psalm 106:12 tells us, **Then believed they his words; they sang his praise.** When the Israelites started believing God's Word, it didn't say they prayed a prayer. When they really got hold of what God's Word says and realized that it belongs to them, they began to sing His praise. When they started believing what God's Word said about anything, they didn't keep on praying. They began to sing praises unto the Lord.

Deuteronomy 10:21 says:

> **He is thy praise, and he is thy God, that hath done for thee these great and terrible things, which thine eyes have seen.**

In this verse, *terrible* means awesome or beyond description. A *praise break* will cause you to visibly see God manifest Himself on your behalf. *Break* means to dig or to plow. Isn't God unique? Hosea 10:11 says, **Judah shall plow.** God spoke to my heart, "Let your praise do your plowing." Your praise not only breaks up fallow ground, but it softens hearts — yours and

27

the hearts of those around you. *Break* means to interrupt or to destroy the continuity or uniformity of something.

Your praise will interrupt and destroy bad habits. It will destroy the uniformity of what the devil keeps bringing to you over and over again or keeps messing with you about. That word *break* means to discontinue abruptly. This means when the enemy begins to tamper with you, your praise will cause him to stop immediately

Every time you open your mouth when the enemy is messing with you, your praise will say, "Stop"! I like that. The word *break* also means to make one's way out of. Praise is going to get you out of some situations. It is going to bring you out of some things you think you can't come out of. It's time for a praise break!

The word *break* also means when something is made known in speech or writing. So our praise will make known in speech to whom we belong. Hosea 11:12 says, **Judah yet ruleth with God.** It means your praise still has power, authority and rulership with God.

I want you to know that your praise is not something you're just doing at home, at church, or in practice. Your praise rules with God. It gets God's attention. And here's the key: Your praise causes God to be **faithful with the saints** (Hosea 11:12).

For you to have this type of partnership with God, you've got to put praise in your mouth. You've got to let praise become a constant partner with you. You've got to interact with praise. When you let praise associate with your lifestyle, be in your lifestyle, in your mouth and in your character, God is faithful.

Faithful means to be strict in the performance of duty. That means whatever it has been designed to do, it will do. Hallelujah! *Faithful* also means it is law to one's promises and you can trust it. When praise is interacting in your mouth and in your life, it is very strict and lord of what is to come to you. It is faithful with the saints who do it. It is made known in speech. The word *break* in relationship to praise also means to impair or weaken in strength, in spirit, in force, or in effect.

Your praise impairs or weakens something. Whatever is holding you in strength, in spirit, in force, your praise is impairing it. That's why Scripture says, **The weapons of our warfare are not carnal, but mighty through God to the pulling down** [weakening and impairing] **of strong holds** (2 Corinthians 10:4).

Your praise weakens those things that are not according to the knowledge of God. You can't keep praising God with nothing about your life changing, nothing about your habits changing, or nothing about your walk changing, because every time you praise God, you impair and weaken the strongholds of the enemy in your life. That's why the greatest weapon that will keep you from backsliding is praise.

You can't be comfortable in doing wrong and saying, "Hallelujah anyhow!" As a pastor, I'm not going to run after people who don't want to live right. I'm not going to miss any sleep over people who are having problems. But I know you can't hang around teaching on praise and worship and not get it together. So keep hanging around with all these hallelujahs, thank You, Jesus, He is Lord, glory to the Lamb, and Hosanna to the King.

In spite of your faults, weaknesses and failures, hang around where praise is going on and after while, we won't have to worry about you hiding anymore. God told me to tell you, "You can't hide anymore."

I will sing to the Lord as long as I live (Psalm 104:33 AMP).

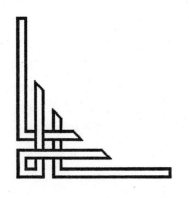

God wants us to take continual praise breaks, just as David did: **I will bless the Lord at all times: his praise shall continually be in my mouth** (Psalm 34:1). *His praise* will be in your mouth instead of problems.

As you become disciplined and trained to take praise breaks, when a problem arises you will say, "I will bless the Lord and not magnify my problem." Every time you tell your problem, you magnify it.

The word *break* also means to be accustomed to a method or procedure. No matter what is going on, you will learn how to give thanks *in* everything, not *for* everything, knowing that this is the will of God in Christ Jesus concerning you. *Break* also means to train away from a habit or a practice. It means to not only discipline and bring into obedience, but also to train your way from a habit or a practice.

Isaiah 61:3 says to put on **the garment of praise for the spirit of heaviness.** God wants to train you away from being sad or weighted down. When things come at you in the natural, instead of having a gloomy day or getting in a tailspin, put off the spirit of heaviness and put on the garment of praise. You have a choice as to which outfit you will wear, so take a praise break!

The last word I picked up about *break* was to free oneself or to escape suddenly. Hebrews 7:14 says, **For it is evident that our Lord sprang out of Juda.** How can we free ourselves and escape suddenly? To get yourself out of a mess quickly, start praising God. If you want to get yourself out of a fix, take a praise break. Scripture says every time Judah is present, our Lord will spring up in it.

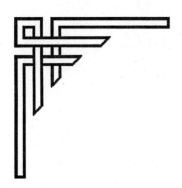

*I will sing of the
mercies
of the Lord for ever
(Psalm 89:1).*

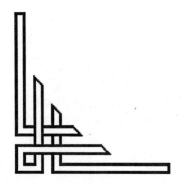

Jeremiah 33:11 says:

> **The voice of joy, and the voice of gladness, the voice of the bridegroom, and the voice of the bride, the voice of them that shall say, Praise the Lord of hosts: for the Lord is good; for his mercy endureth for ever: and of them that shall bring the sacrifice of praise into the house of the Lord. For I will cause to return the captivity of the land, as at the first, saith the Lord.**

Has the enemy been stealing your goods, your peace, joy, prosperity, healing and health? This verse says that if you will bring the sacrifice of praise into the house of the Lord, He will cause the captivity of your land to be given back to you. It's time for a praise break!

Psalm 68:1 says, **Let God arise, let his enemies be scattered.** Verse 19 says, **Blessed be the Lord, who daily loadeth us with benefits.** In addition to salvation, that includes all the things we need, plus the desires of our hearts. **Even the God of our salvation. Selah** (v. 19). In other words, pause and think about it. We are daily loaded with benefits. We need to start praising God for His rule or ownership of everything. He daily loads us with what we need.

Psalm 67:5-7 says:

Let the people praise thee, O God; let all the people praise thee. Praise Him first and He will bless you. **Then shall the earth yield her increase; and God, even our own God, shall bless us** (vv. 5,6). Some increase belongs to you, but it won't be released until you get into praise. **God shall bless us; and all the ends of the earth shall fear him** (v. 7).

This Scripture passage says the blessings will come — God shall bless us — but through *praise*, not through prayer. **God shall bless us.** What a promise! When people see how blessed you are, they are going to say, "I want your God." It's time for a praise break, because God wants to bless His people.

Psalm 35:27 says:

> **Let them shout for joy, and be glad, that favour my right-
> eous cause: yea, let them say continually, Let the Lord be mag-
> nified, which hath pleasure in the prosperity of his servant.**

What does this verse mean? When we begin to praise God,
He leads or directs the prosperity of His people. That means
God takes it upon Himself to see that you prosper. He takes
pleasure in your prosperity. That means He begins to feel this
thing. *Pleasure* means feeling produced by the enjoyment or
expectation of good. It's a state that is agreeable to God, and it
taps His emotions.

When we praise God, we work on God's emotions. Some
people think God doesn't have any feelings, and we've got the
nerve to say, "God, why are You doing this to me?" God has
feelings, and He says, "When you magnify Me, you work on
My feelings, and I make sure you prosper." Take a praise break!
Hallelujah!

You may be questioning, "You mean to tell me, every time
I shout 'Hallelujah!' it really works on God's feelings?" He
says, "I'm telling you that in My Word. Every time you praise
Me and tell Me how great I am, you work on My emotions. I've
got to bless because she says I'm great. I've got to bless her
because she says I'm the King of kings. I've got to bless him
because he keeps saying I'm the Lord of lords. I've got to bless
them because they keep saying, 'You're the Lord of Hosts.' I've
got to bless them! It's time for a praise break!

Psalm 18:1-3 says:

> **I will love thee, O Lord, my strength.**
>
> **The Lord is my rock, my fortress, and my deliverer; my
> God, my strength, in whom I will trust; my buckler, and the
> horn of my salvation, and my high tower.**

I will call upon the Lord, who is worthy to be praised: so shall I be saved from mine enemies.

When I call upon Him and praise Him, I shall be saved from my enemies. Get back, devil! I'm going to be saved, not by saying, "I bind you" or, "I curse you," but by saying, "Jesus, You are so great. There is none like You. You are an awesome God. You are everything to Me. Hallelujah!"

First Samuel 2:1 says:

And Hannah prayed, and said, My heart rejoiceth in the Lord, mine horn is exalted in the Lord: my mouth is enlarged over mine enemies; because I rejoice in thy salvation.

Here's a key for your praise breaks: Don't waste any time by bringing yourself down to your enemies' level by cussing them out. Instead, praise God and let your mouth mount above your enemies. Don't belittle yourself by telling somebody off! God says, "I can't bless you if you are telling people off. I can't bless you giving people a bit of your mind."

God is setting us up. He wants to bless us, so He says to stop everything and take a praise break!

In Psalm 56:1 David said:

Be merciful unto me, O God: for man would swallow me up; he fighting daily oppresseth me.

Did you know you've got some enemies? It may be Mr. or Mrs., Mom or Dad, Grandmother, mother-in-law, or supervisor.

Mine enemies would daily swallow me up: for they be many that fight against me, O thou most High.

Verse 2

It looks like his enemies are coming out of the woodwork.

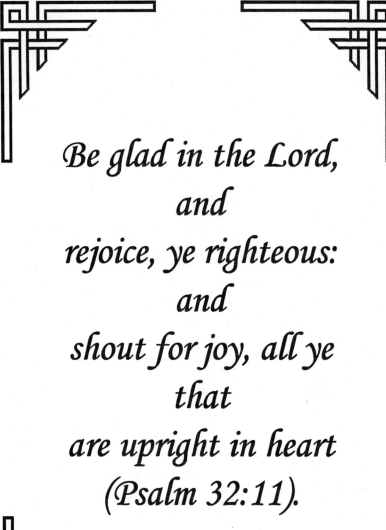

*Be glad in the Lord, and
rejoice, ye righteous:
and
shout for joy, all ye
that
are upright in heart
(Psalm 32:11).*

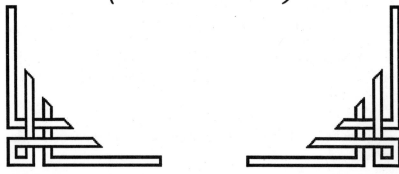

What time I am afraid, *I will trust in thee.*

Verse 3

This means your enemies will try to intimidate you. You won't be exempt from the devil's tactics, but when you are confronted with fear, *elevate your trust*. Trust in God, not in lawyers. Praise Him!

In God I will praise his word, in God I have put my trust; I will not fear what flesh can do unto me.

When I cry unto thee [in praise], then shall mine enemies turn back: this I know; for God is for me.

In God will I praise his word: in the Lord will I praise his word.

In God have I put my trust: I will not be afraid what man can do unto me.

Thy vows are upon me, O God: I will render praises unto thee. [That means take time out for a praise break.]

For thou hast delivered my soul from death: wilt not thou deliver my feet from falling, that I may walk before God in the light of the living?

Psalm 56:4,9-13

It's time for a praise break!

Now, let's look at a portion of Psalm 81:

Sing aloud unto God our strength; make a joyful noise unto the God of Jacob.

For this was a statute for Israel [the Church, the people of God], and a law of the God of Jacob.

Hear, O my people, and I will testify unto thee: O Israel, if thou wilt hearken unto me;

There shall no strange god be in thee; neither shalt thou worship any strange god.

I am the Lord thy God, which brought thee out of the land of Egypt: open thy mouth wide, and I will fill it.

But my people would not hearken to my voice; and Israel would none of me.

So I gave them up unto their own hearts' lust: and they walked in their own counsels.

Oh, that my people had hearkened unto me, and Israel had walked in my ways!

I should soon have subdued their enemies, and turned my hand against their adversaries.

The haters of the Lord should have submitted themselves unto him: but their time should have endured for ever.

He should have fed them also with the finest of the wheat: and with honey out of the rock should I have satisfied thee.

Psalm 81:1,4,8-16

If we will become doers of God's Word, He will subdue our enemies before our face, and they will have to submit to the God in us!

I believe God is saying, "You think you are getting the Word now, but I've got the finest of the wheat. I've got some revelation that I want to give you, and take you to another level spiritually. What looks like a hard place for you now, in the midst of your hardness, in the midst of your toughness, in the midst of your problems or circumstances which seem immovable, I'm going to give you honey out of it.

"I'm going to take what the enemy has sent to destroy you and weigh you down and keep you down and allow the sweetness of it to come out of it to satisfy you so you can be like

Joseph. What the enemy meant for evil, God worked for good. God is going to take your hard time, and you're going to start licking your lips! You'll taste honey out of the Rock!"

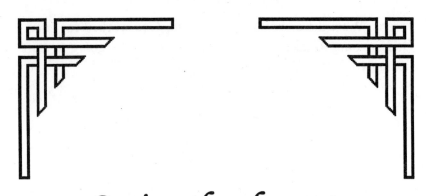

*O give thanks unto
the Lord;
for he is good:
because his
mercy endureth for
ever
(Psalm 118:1).*

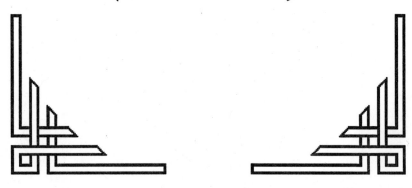

4
Identifying Your Enemies

Second Chronicles, chapter 20, verse 1, says:

It came to pass after this also, that the children of Moab, and the children of Ammon, and with them other beside the Ammonites, came against Jehoshaphat to battle.

In the second verse, it tells us that these enemies that came against them were **a great multitude...in Hazazon-tamar, which is Engedi.** We're going to break these words down so they will mean something to you about your praise. At this time, Jehoshaphat was the king of Judah. The enemy had sent a great multitude against the tribe of Judah.

The Moabite Spirit

The *spirit of the Moabites* represents idolatry. Anything you put before God can become an idol. It doesn't have to be a golden image. Some of us don't have enough gold to melt down to make one. But that image can be human, it can be your job, your children, or your mate. Anything that takes top priority with you and comes between you and your time with God is idolatry. The Moabite spirit came against the children of Judah to bring them poverty. The spirit of Moabite is poverty — barely making it from paycheck to paycheck.

Superstition is another characteristic of the Moabites. Some people still believe in black cats or in the old cliche, "If you

break a mirror or glass, you'll have seven years of bad luck."
You wonder if that's really true. I'm going to tell you, it's not.
I don't care what your Grandma said or your Aunt Maggie.
There's no Scripture that tells you that when you break a mirror
or a glass, you'll have seven years of bad luck. Or when you see
a black cat cross your path, it's bad luck. Your right hand itch-
es, your left eye jumps. That's the Moabite spirit. Superstition!

God doesn't need your hands to itch for you to believe what
you're going to do. He doesn't need your right eye to jump when
you're going to be happy and your left eye to jump when you're
going to be sad. You either have dry skin in the palm of your
hand, or a nerve problem. That's what's going on with the eye.

Another sign of the Moabite spirit is, nothing seems to satisfy you. When you don't have anything in the natural that sat-
isfies you, you go outside of what God's Word says to get satisfaction. That's the Moabite spirit. Being in the Lord is not
enough satisfaction for you.

Another characteristic of the Moabite spirit is pride. It's one
thing to know who you are in Christ, it's another thing to think
you are something in the natural. There are certain people you
want to identify with. That's the Moabite spirit.

The Moabite spirit fought Israel and Judah. They were in
constant war with Judah, the praisers, and with Israel, the
Church. If you don't learn how to worship God as Judah did,
then praise will never be in Israel, the Church. If Judah hadn't
praised God, then Israel would never have become praisers.

The Moabite spirit always wants to marry people in the
church and manifest its character attributes of idolatry, wealth,
poverty, superstition, lack of satisfaction and pride.

If you rob God of tithes and offerings, you'll always have
poverty. When you feel you can't afford to tithe, you are mar-

ried to the Moabite spirit. If you have something speaking to you and it doesn't sound like the Spirit of God, get rid of it. The Moabite spirit fights believers, because it doesn't want you to get to your promised land.

It will try to keep you looking after other things to satisfy you, to put things before God and His Word, to keep you poor, defeated and unsatisfied. It refuses to let you pass into your promised land.

The Midianite Spirit

The Moabite spirit always joins with other spirits, like it did in the Bible, to fight against Judah and the Israelites. One of the spirits it joined up with was *the Midianite spirit,* which is a judgmental spirit. The people who don't praise and worship God usually have this spirit. They are critical and judgmental.

Someone with a Midianite spirit always finds others who aren't living right. They can see everybody else's problems, and they find fault with the leader and everything else in the house. Nothing goes right for them in the church. It's because they are courting a Moabite spirit.

The Midianite spirit will make you see church people wrong. You'll even begin making statements such as, "You know, the church used to love everybody, but now they don't love." So what's wrong with your love? If the church doesn't love like they should, why don't you love like you should?

First Peter 4:8 says, **And above all things have fervent charity** [love] **among yourselves: for charity shall cover the multitude of sins.** If you're seeing no love, that means you don't have any because your love will go past what you think people feel about you.

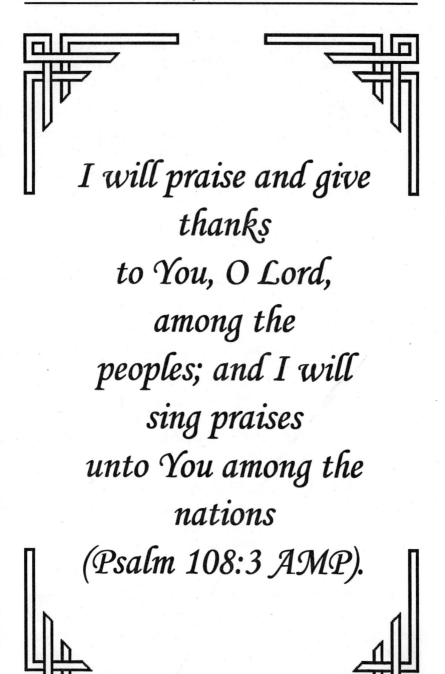

I will praise and give thanks
to You, O Lord,
among the
peoples; and I will
sing praises
unto You among the
nations
(Psalm 108:3 AMP).

The Midianite spirit will cause you to judge people by your own emotions or circumstances. It's easy to bring this spirit into the church if you're not praising God.

You just got in a fight with your husband or wife, everybody at home is mad, and your dog and cat are fighting each other, so when you come into the church and you don't feel good yourself, you think everybody else is fighting you. Yet people aren't even paying attention to you. You tell yourself, "Sister So-and-so passed right by me." She was probably running late and didn't even see you.

I want you to understand the groundwork of the Moabite and the Midianite spirits, because 2 Kings 3:8-27 says these spirits — idolatry, poverty, superstition, dissatisfaction, pride, criticalness and judgmentalism — can be conquered by the Church and Judah. So if you are hanging out in any of these areas, you can be conquered! But the Spirit of God in you can conquer any of these things that torment you.

The Word of God tells us in 2 Samuel 8:2-12 that the Moabite spirit was defeated by David, and we've got the spirit of David.

Praise will break a whole lot of your habits off of you. Order your steps to walk upright, because the Moabite spirit was defeated by David. That means you can defeat it, too.

The Amorite Spirit

Now, let's look at another spirit, *the Amorite spirit*, whose characteristics are cruelty, pride, carelessness and idolatry. It loves to team up with the Moabite spirit.

Are you beginning to understand why God wants us to take on the spirit of praise? I've said many times, you cannot be a believer and a worshipper and still be mean and hateful. You cannot remain a praiser and a worshipper and still be telling people off. You cannot remain a praiser and a worshipper and not know how to talk to people. You just can't worship God one minute and be nasty the next.

If you're still dealing with some of these negative characteristics, you need to rise up with the spirit of praise on your lips and kill those qualities.

To tell someone off will simply let them know that the spirit of the enemy resides in you. Now, I am fully aware that all of us will have several opportunities, as long as we live, to tell people off. The enemy sets people up intentionally to mess with us. We have to fight with the Amorite spirit all the time because we're in the world but not of the world.

As we begin to reign as kings and priests as God intends, then we'll know how to get the enemy off of our back because the praisers in Scripture ran him off. Praise will keep us from getting out of the anointing.

Remember, when you get saved, a spirit of amnesia doesn't come over you. You don't forget how to use those foreign words. Things will come up that sound mighty nice to tell people a thing or two. As much as I love God, there are times I try to tell God, "If You just let me tell them." We don't want people to think we'll take just anything, you know, but the Lord will give you wisdom on how to deal with people and even the right words.

We need to never think ourselves to be above anyone. I'm glad that spirit doesn't rest in my church, because we have people from different backgrounds, cultures, races and status.

Because you've got $10 more than I've got doesn't make you more important. We are not to be hung up with titles and positions. The only position that we should be hung up over is our position in Christ Jesus. We don't have to push our authority or prove who we are. I know who I am. I don't have to go around and remind any other woman that I'm married to Luther. I don't have to be with Luther twenty-four hours a day for him to know I'm married to him.

God is calling us to a praise break, because the higher we go in Him, the greater the war. It's time for us to come to a rest in worship and let the Lord of Hosts do battle for us. That's what He wants

The Chaldean Spirit

In 2 Kings, chapter 24, we find a group of people called *the Chaldees*, who believed in horoscopes, witchcraft and zodiac signs. This type of spirit hangs out, and it is nothing to play around with. A believer should not walk around with a zodiac sign around his neck. His or her signs are the blood of Jesus and the cross. We read some of these things and say, "That sounds just like me." That's why they call it horoscope. I've had callers to our ministry ask, "What sign were you born under?" I tell them, "*The cross.*" That's a believer's sign. Behind horoscopes and zodiac signs are evil spirits that will hinder your worship of God. This is why God is calling believers to a praise break.

Have you ever felt lonely at times and things have gotten a little tough? You've tried to believe God, yet it looks like nothing is happening. You lie in the bed at night crying and saying, "God, when are You going to get me out of this?"

All at once a psychic comes on TV and says, "You were abused at age seven." "Yeah, that's right!" (You didn't know it.) "Your daddy left you at age ten." "Yeah." "You are getting ready to go into a new career." "Yeah, that's right, I just got hired." You say, "Maybe I should just call the psychic hot line. It won't mean a thing to me because I believe You, God, but I'd like to see what they have to say."

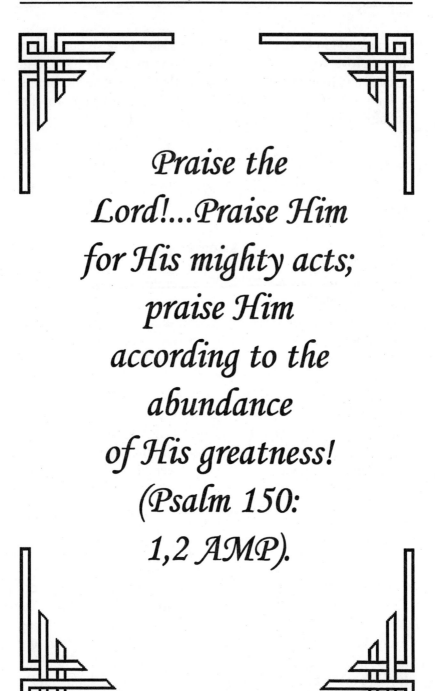

Praise the Lord!...Praise Him for His mighty acts; praise Him according to the abundance of His greatness! (Psalm 150: 1,2 AMP).

So, for 75 cents a minute, you call the psychic hot line. The psychic tells you, "I see that you have been rejected." That's right, you've been rejected. Anyone who has lived in this world any amount of time is going to experience rejection. It is nothing new under the sun. We're all going to be rejected in some form or another. If your daddy likes you, your mother may not like you. If your daddy and mother both love you, you may have a brother or a sister who doesn't like you. You're going to experience rejection, so you *don't* need a psychic to tell you that

You're going to have some hard times. The Bible says, **Many are the afflictions of the righteous: but the Lord delivereth him out of them all** (Psalm 34:19). You may be experiencing affliction right now, or you may be going through a difficulty. It looks like God hasn't come through for you. It's time for a praise break!

As I was studying about these spirits that come up against people, I read that the Amorites hired people to fight against David. (See 2 Chronicles, chapter 10.)

Stopping These Spirits With Your Generation

Now, let's look at Deuteronomy 23:3-5 to see what God is speaking to us:

> **An Ammonite or Moabite shall not enter into the congregation of the Lord; even to their tenth generation shall they not enter into the congregation of the Lord for ever:**

> **Because they met you not with bread and with water in the way, when ye came forth out of Egypt; and because they hired against thee Balaam the son of Beor of Pethor of Mesopotamia, to curse thee.**

Nevertheless the Lord thy God would not hearken unto Balaam; but the Lord thy God turned the curse into a blessing unto thee, because the Lord thy God loved thee.

We just got through talking about the Moabites and Amorites. It says that they shall not enter the congregation of the Lord. This is a message to you and me in this hour: *Don't bring your cruelty, pride, idolatry, superstition, pride and vindictiveness into the house of the Lord.* These spirits must be stopped from working in our lives and in the lives of our households. Otherwise, they will be passed down from generation to generation.

You cannot act any kind of way, be any kind of person you want to be and do anything you want to do with your worship life. Everything that you encounter — idolatry, superstition, cruelty and poverty — will either stop with you, or it will carry down to your tenth generation. You need to say, "Enemy, you're stopping right here and right now, in Jesus' name." These things will drop off of you as you allow a praise break to become a normal part of your daily lifestyle. Hallelujah!

It's not normal to be hateful, up and down in your emotions like a roller coaster, or to have consistent pity parties. It's not normal to be a complainer or a murmurer. It's not normal that you make up any kind of excuse in your walk with God as to why you can't obey Him.

You would be surprised at some of the things I hear about people. "I haven't been to church in a long time, because I've just been having problems with myself." Well, where are you supposed to be? Church is not for perfect people. It's for people to come and get to know their God. So if we don't stop these spirits in our praise break, they will be carried down to future generations.

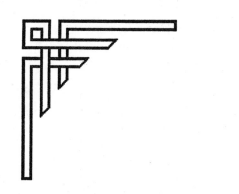
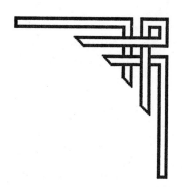

*One generation
shall praise
thy works to
another, and
shall declare thy
mighty acts
(Psalm 145:4).*

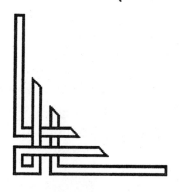

A house that teaches about worship will experience some warfare but the praise and worship will bring breakthroughs. You may be saying, "God, I'm really trying to believe You. Miracles are flying above my head, but they haven't stopped at my house yet. The more I'm believing You, it looks like hell's breaking loose from every direction. But in reality, though I may not see it yet, heaven is breaking loose."

Your praise and worship make the enemy angry at you. That's why you'll come up against some opposition, but so what? The battle is not yours, but it's the Lord's.

Scripture says the Amorites and the Moabites should not enter into the congregation because they met you not with bread and water in the way. They're not coming to satisfy you, they're coming to destroy you when you come forth out of Egypt (bondage).

Let's look at verse 5 of Deuteronomy, chapter 23, again:

> **Nevertheless the Lord thy God would not hearken unto Balaam; but *the Lord thy God turned the curse into a blessing unto thee*, because the Lord thy God loved thee.**

God said that He would turn the curse. In spite of what the enemy is attempting to do to you, just take a praise break, because God is going to turn the curse into a blessing. God's getting ready to turn this thing. Your praise will quicken the turn of events in your life.

Now, I'm not the solution to any of your problems. But I'm trying to point you to the Deliverer. When trials, challenges, troubles and disappointments come up against you, go to God. You've got to take the Word and get violent with the devil. You can say, "If God said it, I'm going to hang in there, whatever it costs me. I don't care how the storm may blow. I'm still going to hang in there and believe God and the promises of His Word."

"Well, Pastor, I'm at the end of my rope." Tie a knot and hang on! Hang in there! It's time for a praise break! God is going to turn your curse into a blessing because of His love for you. God takes pleasure in our praise. He gets excited when we praise Him.

5
The Battle Is the Lord's

In 2 Chronicles, chapter 20, these enemies came against Jehoshaphat. The first step to take is found in verse 3: **And Jehoshaphat feared, and set himself to seek the Lord, and proclaimed a fast throughout all Judah.** Get in the face of God.

And Judah gathered themselves together... (v. 4). As a church, it's time to gather ourselves together. It's time for us to seek God's glory. It's no time to nitpick. If you've got some people who still want to nitpick, let them. If you have someone who's always getting up front and you find out they have been offended, put them up front until they can grow beyond it. Do anything you can to be your brother's keeper until they grow up.

Judah took a stand and in the face of the enemy said, "We're in this thing together." Never rejoice over anyone's downfall or failure. Proverbs 24:17 says, **Rejoice not when thine enemy falleth, and let not thine heart be glad when he stumbleth.**

Don't ever let yourself feel like you're so strong you'll never go down. The late Mother Teresa said, "Never look down on anybody until you're ready to pick them up." That's the only time to look down on someone: When you're looking down to pick them up!

Judah came together in a fast and asked the Lord to help

them. Then Jehoshaphat, the leader, stood in the congregation and began to pray. Look at the prayer he prayed as a praise: **Art not thou God in heaven? and rulest not thou over all the kingdoms of the heathen?** (2 Chronicles 20:6). He wasn't saying, "God, what are You going to do?" He was reminding himself in praise Who God was.

> **In thine hand is there not power and might, so that none is able to withstand thee?**
>
> **Art not thou our God, who didst drive out the inhabitants of this land before thy people Israel, and gavest it to the seed of Abraham thy friend for ever?**
>
> **Verses 6,7**

We need to start praying this prayer for ourselves.

> **And they dwelt therein, and have built thee a sanctuary therein for thy name, saying,**
>
> **If, when evil cometh upon us as a sword, judgment, or pestilence, or famine, we stand before this house, and in thy presence, (for thy name is in this house,) and cry unto thee in our affliction, then thou wilt hear and help.**
>
> **And now, behold** [he began to name the enemies that came against them], **the children of Ammon and Moab and mount Seir, whom thou wouldest not let Israel invade, when they came out of the land of Egypt.**
>
> **Verses 8-10**

The Lord wouldn't let Israel invade when they came out of the land of Egypt, because they didn't know how to deal with their flesh. That's why some of us were so happy and full of joy when we got saved. You wanted the whole world and you didn't even have any problems. It looked like all your sins disappeared for two weeks. "I decided to follow Jesus." "You mean you left Jim and his broad shoulders, Mary with her cocoa shape, the bottle, the pipe and the joint?" You said, "I'm finished. I've decided to follow Jesus, no turning back."

You wanted church. "Pastor, can we have a service tonight?" No, we don't have a service. "Well, I feel we should have one. Something has happened to me way down on the inside from the top of my head to the soles of my feet. I'm just so happy with Jesus."

In about two weeks it looks like somebody let the air out of the bag. Someone calls and asks you, "Where are you?" "I just got a little bit discouraged. My old drinking buddy showed back up on my doorstep. I thought I was delivered, but when he showed back up...." You see, you have to deal with your flesh.

"I just went to my friend's housewarming party. I said, 'I don't touch that anymore, God saved me.' They know I don't drink now, but they just kept passing that stuff in front of me. And Pastor, the thermometer in the house was set at 85. They had it so hot and I was sweating. They didn't have any air conditioner, and this ice cold Blue Ribbon used to quench my taste. I don't know what happened, but they all left to fix their plates in the kitchen. I was still left and I just kind of walked past, and the next thing I knew, all their glasses were empty!"

If I didn't have to keep the secrets of people's hearts, I could write a book that the angels would take a break and start laughing!

After Jehoshaphat and all Judah petitioned the Lord, the Spirit of the Lord came on the Prophet Jahaziel and he said:

> **Hearken ye, all Judah, and ye inhabitants of Jerusalem, and thou king Jehoshaphat, Thus saith the Lord unto you, Be not afraid nor dismayed by reason of this great multitude; for the battle is not yours, but God's.**

> **2 Chronicles 20:15**

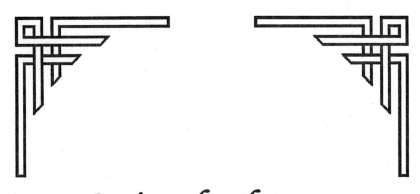

*O give thanks unto
the Lord,
call upon His name,
make known His
doings among the
peoples!
(Psalm 105:1 AMP).*

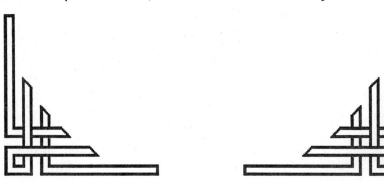

God is speaking this same message to you and me. Every time we decree God's getting ready to take us to the next level, we have a famine in the church.

When I ministered in Atlanta, Georgia, a lady from Liberia, Africa, prophesied almost word for word what God is doing for people in our church. Ever since that word, I have decreed that every need in my church is met. Yet, in the natural, we wonder if we are going to make it another week. The enemy tries to bring worry just as he did with King Jehoshaphat about the great multitude of enemies.

But thank God, His grace is sufficient. We're still going to be on prime time TV. God is still going to elevate many in the house. God is going to make millionaires of many sitting in the midst of us. God has got some people who are going to be faithful to His stewardship so He can show Himself strong on their behalf. God is still going to save households. God is still God!

All God wants of us is for us to take praise breaks every day. Regardless of what kind of enemy comes against your family, take a praise break. I don't care what it looks like, it's time for a praise break. It's no time to be sad or despondent. Take a praise break!

The Lord has spoken, **Be not afraid nor dismayed by reason of this great multitude;** *for the battle is not yours, but God's* (2 Chronicles 20:15). **Be not afraid nor dismayed** means get up and stop feeling sorry for yourself. Don't call my number, and don't call anybody else's number. God put this word in Scripture because there will be times when we will have an opportunity to become fearful. There will be times when we have an opportunity to be dismayed, fainthearted and lose courage. But take a praise break instead, for the battle is not ours, but the Lord's.

Bless the Lord, O my soul: and all that is within me, bless his holy name (Psalm 103:1).

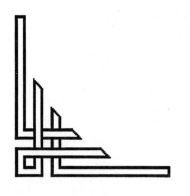

To morrow go ye down against them (v. 16) means *rise up, go and conquer!*

Ye shall not need to fight in this battle: set yourselves, stand ye still, and see the salvation of the Lord with you... (v. 17). "Set yourself" with a praise break! **Fear not, nor be dismayed; to morrow go out against them: for the Lord will be with you** (v. 17).

And Jehoshaphat bowed his head with his face to the ground: and all Judah and the inhabitants of Jerusalem fell before the Lord, worshipping the Lord.

Verse 18

We heard the voice of the Lord telling us about victory for us. The land is ours and God is going to put us on display. We have shouted and now it's time to worship.

Jehoshaphat and the children of Judah praised in the midst of the enemy still surrounding them. It wasn't just noise. These people stood up and praised God while the enemy was still encircling them. In the midst of this, their faith took them into a high praise. They rose up and Jehoshaphat said, **Believe in the Lord your God, so shall ye be established; believe his prophets, so shall ye prosper** (v. 20).

We have been set up to prosper because we believe in the prophets of God. We can't go under because we're part of the covenant. The prophets of God shall say we are a blessed people. People are coming from the north, the south, the east and the west. There will be no room to hold all these people. They shall come as households and by generations. Not only shall we get the heathens, but we're going to get their treasures! We believe in the prophets of God and we shall prosper.

And when he [Jehoshaphat] had consulted with the people, he appointed singers unto the Lord, and that should praise the beauty of holiness, as they went out before the army, and to say,

Praise the Lord; for his mercy endureth for ever.

And when they began to sing and to praise, the Lord set ambushments against [their enemies]....

2 Chronicles 20:21,22

They took a praise break: *"Praise the Lord, for his mercy endureth for ever."* When you begin to sing and to praise, the Lord will set up ambushments against your enemies.

Jehoshaphat and the people of Judah were already defeated in numbers. You may be defeated and everything around you seems to be caving in. But as you begin to sing and to praise God, the enemy will turn on themselves, just as they did with Jehoshaphat and the children of Judah.

Remember, the battle is not yours, but the Lord's. You don't have to worry about calling anybody up and telling them. Just sing and praise. Take a praise break.

As you let praise be continually in your mouth, the Lord will set ambushments against your enemy and the enemy will turn against themselves. The enemy will come after you one way and flee seven ways (Deuteronomy 28:7). The Lord will turn this thing around, but He will do it when you take a praise break!

This is no time to stop, lay at home and lick your wounds. Bring your wounds and all to the congregation of the righteous and get up. When the children of Judah got to the enemy, they were all dead. They left their gold, their silver and their precious jewels, and all they did was praise God. By the time they got to the place where the enemy was, the word of the Lord said they gathered the spoils and it took three days to do it (v. 25).

It's time to pick up the spoils from battle and rejoice! Take another praise break and celebrate, thanking the Lord for turning your captivity, similar to that recorded in Psalm 126:1-3:

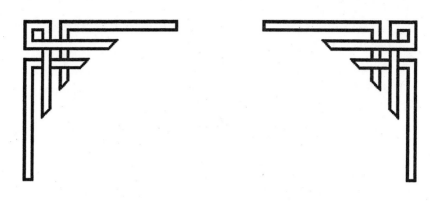

O give thanks unto the Lord; call upon his name: make known his deeds among the people (Psalm 105:1).

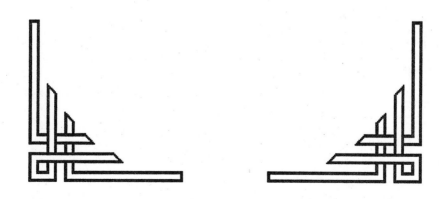

When the Lord turned again the captivity of Zion, we were like them that dream.

Then was our mouth filled with laughter, and our tongue with singing: then said they among the heathen, The Lord hath done great things for them.

The Lord hath done great things for us; whereof we are glad.

6

You've Been Down and Out Long Enough!

Out of the mouth of babes and sucklings [he's talking about the newborn, Spirit-filled creations of God] **hast thou ordained** [or ordered] **strength....**

Psalm 8:2

The word *strength* in the Hebrew means "praise." What is God's purpose for praise? **Because of thine enemies, that thou mightest still the enemy and the avenger** (v. 2). God has ordained praise to come out of your mouth because of your enemy.

When the enemy rages, take a praise break. I'm going to put the praise of God in my mouth and watch Him put a muzzle on the enemy.

Deuteronomy 28:32 says:

Thy sons and thy daughters shall be given unto another people, and thine eyes shall look, and fail with longing for them all the day long: and there shall be no might in thine hand.

Are you tired of the enemy messing around with your children, and you can't seem to do anything about it? Are you tired of the enemy messing with you, and it looks like you can't get yourself out of it?

"I'm working all day long and half of the week I work overtime, and I still can't seem to prosper." **The fruit of thy land, and all thy labours, shall a nation which thou knowest not eat up...** (v. 33). I'm not planning on that!

You're asking, "You mean to tell me it's possible for another person to eat up my fruit and my labor? I'm going to work hard and not enjoy it? I'm going to save up and not be able to enjoy it? I'm going to work all year long and not get a vacation? I can't afford a vacation. I've got to beg the man, "Can I work during my vacation, because I still need to make ends meet?" You should be swelling up with anger if something like that is happening in your life.

And thou shalt be only oppressed and crushed alway (v. 33). Do you plan on living like that? You can wear oppression only so long until you start showing it. This Scripture goes on to other things, such as serving other gods, but look at verse 38:

> **Thou shalt carry much seed out in the field, and shalt gather but little in; for the locust shall consume it.**

The word *locust*, as it's used here, means famine, lack of jobs, recession and hard times.

"You mean to tell me I'm going to carry much seed out, put seed in the ground and the locusts are going to consume it? Or, I'm going to put seed in, and then right away I'm going to be laid off from my job and won't have a chance to harvest because I eat up my seed?"

> **Thou shalt plant vineyards, and dress them** [have savings bonds and investments]**, but shalt neither drink of the wine, nor gather the grapes** [before they become wine]**; for the worms shall eat them.**

Verse 39

You may be in a position where you haven't even planted

the vineyard, let alone dressed it or eaten of it.

Thou shalt have olive trees throughout all thy coasts [represents wealth], but thou shalt not anoint thyself with oil....

Verse 40

You can't even go on a cruise. You're working and you can't do anything. You would like to go to Red Lobster, but you don't have the money. "Is there any special going on where two can eat for the price of one? I just can't afford to buy myself a steak." That's the time you should buy your biggest steak!

Thou shalt have olive trees...but thou shalt not anoint thyself with the oil; for thine olive shall cast his fruit.

Thou shalt beget sons and daughters, but thou shalt not enjoy them; for they shall go into captivity.

All the trees and fruit of thy land shall the locust consume.

The stranger that is within thee shall get up above thee very high; and thou shalt come down very low.

Verses 40-43

What spirit are you operating under? Sometimes "the stranger" is our family. If we're not careful, we let the enemy in our family bring us down. There is a time we've got to love, and there is a time we've got to have tough love. I refuse to let the enemy through the stranger of my seed or through a friend bring me down low.

He shall lend to thee, and thou shalt not lend to him....

Verse 44

If you're forty-five years old and you still get a $10 allowance, the devil is a liar! You're working and can't spend your own money? You may be under that type of bondage and a stranger is lending to you.

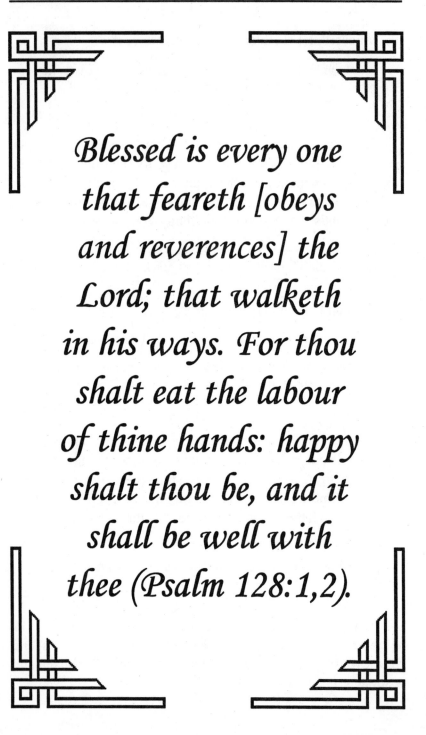

*Blessed is every one
that feareth [obeys
and reverences] the
Lord; that walketh
in his ways. For thou
shalt eat the labour
of thine hands: happy
shalt thou be, and it
shall be well with
thee (Psalm 128:1,2).*

What's in my billfold or in my purse is mine! If I care to share it, I will. "Bring all of your money home, and I'll issue out your allowance." Tell somebody, "You don't want to go there!" The devil is a liar!

Or a spouse says, "I wear the pants." Take a praise break! That's the stranger within! "I'm the boss. I write out the checks." Take a praise break!

He shall lend to thee, and thou shalt not lend to him (v. 44) because you don't have anything. The enemy has taken it. **He shall be the head, and thou shalt be the tail** (v. 44). The devil is a liar. Take a praise break!

Since we're talking about this stranger, I might as well tell you, there's no such thing as, "Honey, can I go to the store?" He buys you a pager and a cellular phone so he can call you every hour. You're the tail and he's the head. That's in the Book! You're driving down the road, haven't even been to the store for forty-five minutes and you get a call. "Where are you now?" Take a praise break!

I'm not just talking about the women's side. Some men, bless their hearts, are in bad shape. "I've got to take all my paycheck home to my wife, because if I don't give it to her, she won't be a wife." Take a praise break!

Among the curses listed in Deuteronomy 28:15-68, it talks about diseases and other things coming upon you.

> **Moreover all these curses shall come upon thee, and shall pursue thee, and overtake thee, till thou be destroyed; because thou hearkenedst not unto the voice of the Lord thy God, to keep his commandments and his statutes which he commanded thee:**
>
> **And they shall be upon thee for a sign and for a wonder, and upon thy seed for ever.**
>
> **Deuteronomy 28:45,46**

The way you let the enemy do you now is going to pass down to your children. If you're letting the devil walk all over you and do you any kind of way, your children are going to reap the same type of fruit. Women, if you've been dogged out by men, and just can't be your own self, it will be passed down to your seed, and vice versa. The way the enemy makes you poor, broke, miserable, unhappy and depressed is going to be passed down to your seed.

Your children see you having a pity party, and sometimes you wonder why they act the way they do. They are reaping *your attitudes*! In many cases, your children are disobedient because you are disobedient to God. How can you expect your children to walk in submission to your authority when you don't walk in submission to the God of all authority?

The centurion is a good example of a man who is in sub-mission to authority:

> **I am not worthy that thou shouldest come under my roof: but speak the word only, and my servant shall be healed.**
>
> **For *I am a man under authority*, having soldiers under me: and I say to this man, Go, and he goeth; and to another, Come, and he cometh; and to my servant, Do this, and he doeth it.**
>
> **Matthew 8:8,9**

As a parent, check out your own obedience to God. If your children are restless, it's not the sugar from a candy bar. It's your own spirit that you display in the home that makes your children restless. You can't sit around in the home and talk about people, and criticize the pastor and your church without your children displaying that same spirit. It's time for a praise break!

This is why I made up my mind that I will not be the advo-cate of a poverty situation. Even though I grew up in it, somebody has to break this thing, and I made up my mind that if it takes all that I've got in the natural, I'm going to believe God in spite of it. I came from a family who lived from paycheck to paycheck, and sometimes we didn't even know there was a paycheck in the house. You think I want my children to come under that same mess? I know that God can bring deliverance and cause change from generation to generation.

Scripture says:

> **...for I the Lord thy God am a jealous God, visiting the iniquity of the fathers upon the children unto the third and fourth generation of them that hate me,**
>
> **And shewing mercy unto thousands of them that love me and keep my commandments.**
>
> **Deuteronomy 5:9,10**

I want God's blessing and prosperity and peace to be upon me so it can go on down to my seed and to succeeding generations. I am fighting the good fight of faith. God has given us a way out. Look around and you will discover that your own way hasn't worked.

God says:

> **...I have set before you life and death, blessing and cursing: therefore choose life, that both thou and thy seed may live.**
>
> **Deuteronomy 30:19**

You want your children to be the best, yet you ask, "How come my kids can't make good grades in school?" Do you pass the tests that God gives you? Try passing God's tests. See that the spirit of excellence gets in your children and is passed down to your seed

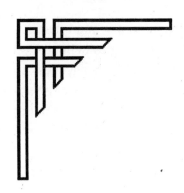

Through God we shall do valiantly, for He it is Who shall tread down our adversaries (Psalm 60:12 AMP).

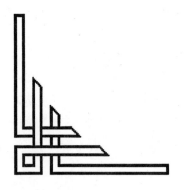

Once you have been exposed to the Word and you don't do it is a very dangerous thing. It would be better for you never to have heard it. But once you've heard it and choose not to do it, that will put you in warfare with the enemy. In my church only the Word is taught, so the enemy always comes immediately to try to steal the seed of the Word so you won't get a harvest. But the devil is a liar.

> **And they [these curses] shall be upon thee for a sign and for a wonder, and upon thy seed for ever.**
>
> **Because thou servedst not the Lord thy God with joyfulness, and with gladness of heart, for the abundance of all things.**
>
> **Deuteronomy 28:46,47**

As a Christian you should not be coming into the church and worshipping the Lord, then have a sad attitude and be crying the blues in your daily life. If God said that we can be joyful, that means we have the capacity and the ability to be joyful all the time. If He said to put on the garment of praise for the spirit of heaviness, that means we can do it. It's our choice. But if we choose to be sad and get wrinkles in our face, then we are in danger, because it will hinder our ability to worship God with joyfulness and gladness of heart.

There are times I wish I could go down a road, down an alley, and out into the community and just plaster smiles on people!

You would be surprised how gorgeous you look when you smile. You would be surprised the horror that I see when I stand up in the pulpit. Frankenstein doesn't have anything on some of the expressions! By the way, there is no "holy" look. If someone told you there is a holy look, that's a lie. There is no holy look, but there is a command in the Word to "be holy."

Great is our Lord,
and of great
power: his under-
standing is infinite
(Psalm 147:5).

Because you did not serve the Lord with joyfulness and gladness of heart for the things that He has already done, verse 48 of Deuteronomy, chapter 28, says:

> **Therefore shalt thou serve thine enemies which the Lord shall send against thee, in hunger, and in thirst, and in nakedness, and in want of all things: and he shall put a yoke of iron upon thy neck, until he have destroyed thee.**

Hunger and thirst, never being satisfied, never getting the desires of your heart, never getting what you want are enemies. To not eat of the good of the land, the fruit of your seed, the harvest and the vineyard, are enemies.

God wants us to get to the place where we receive the desires of our hearts. I used to think beans were for poor people, because when we didn't have anything growing up, we knew we had pinto beans and cornbread. But listen, that's a treat because there's a whole lot of protein in beans. But you should be able to eat what you want to eat, the fullness of God, both naturally and spiritually.

Dissatisfaction and nakedness are enemies. If it's wintertime and you can't afford a pair of boots, that's a dangerous enemy. To know that you need something and can't get it is an enemy. To not have proper clothing for the season is nakedness. It's an enemy.

Do you have someone around you who begs all the time? "Give me fifty cents." "I'm a little short, got a quarter?" "You got a dollar so I can finish this up?" "If I could just have a couple more dollars." "No, I don't have enough money to go there." "We're going to run down to McDonalds. How much is a Happy Meal?" "No, sir, Big Whopper." "Give me the Jr. Whopper." "See how much change I've got in this cigarette tray. Is that another quarter? Look under the seat. One fell out of my purse, but I didn't pick it up."

"Hello, Mary, do you have three eggs? I want to finish making a cake. I just need about a half cup of sugar, that's all." "I'm getting ready to go to my friend's graduation. Can I borrow your car?" "Excuse me, do you have a spare 19-inch rim?" I'm talking about when you don't have a spare tire and you've got a flat, you're calling somebody to get another spare. It sounds comical, but you're in want of things, and God is trying to get us into an area of a praise break so these things can be released to us.

In verse 48, the **yoke of iron upon thy neck** refers to heaviness or being weighted down. You can't get up or you can't get to the stature that you should be. He will allow a yoke of iron to be around your neck until it has destroyed you. But God said, "I have ordained praise to get you released from this!" God has ordered praise. You can't see your way through? God has ordered praise! You've been down and out long enough. God is ordering praise!

Psalm 137:1 says, **By the rivers of Babylon, there we sat down.** *Babylon* is always symbolic of bondage. Some of you have sat down by the rivers and a whole lot of things have you in captivity — sickness, oppression, your job and family. You've thought, "Whatever my lot may be." God didn't order it! Yes, there will be some valleys, but we're not supposed to set up camp there. We're supposed to walk through the valley, not go there and live. God is ready and willing to bring His Word to pass in your life. It's time to get up and take a praise break!

If you sit down by the rivers of Babylon, guess what you will bring in? Sadness. "God, You know, if my mother would have just been here today. Won't anybody else be with me, God? I miss my mother so much." There's no friend like a mom.

"When did she die?" "Forty years ago." I know you miss

your mom, because I've experienced that, but after awhile you should be able to get up. "I don't know where to go because I married when I was nineteen years old. We had a good marriage, we bought our home and cars, and I helped my husband go through school. Then he turned around and helped me to go through school. When he got promoted, he left me." It's time to get up and take a praise break!

"My son went the wrong way. I just can't do anything with him. He got in trouble, and it's my fault. Maybe if I would have given him the car when he was sixteen, he never would have stolen a car." It's time to take a praise break!

We can sit down and feel sorry for ourselves, but God wants to bring us out of it. "Well, Pastor, you don't understand. I was nine years old when I was molested by my daddy, then by my step-daddy, an uncle, and after my uncle, my granddaddy, one after the other. I just feel like I am nothing." Get up from the rivers of Babylon because what the enemy meant for evil, God will turn it around and work it together for your good. Whoever God cleanses is cleansed. There are no dirty people in God.

No, I don't know what you've experienced, but you don't know what I've experienced either. Something I have just encountered I don't think you could handle it. Sometimes I have to brace myself and say, "I'm not preaching about Pat's prosperity. I'm not preaching about healing because I have none. But I can preach about God, because His Word says, **And they went forth, and preached every where, the Lord working with them, confirming the word with signs following** (Mark 16:20)."

This is why I'm telling you, I'm not staying by the rivers of Babylon. God has ordained praise.

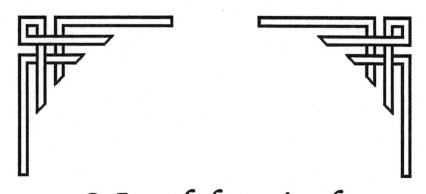

O Israel, hope in the Lord! For with the Lord there is mercy and loving-kindness, and with Him is plenteous redemption (Psalm 130:7 AMP).

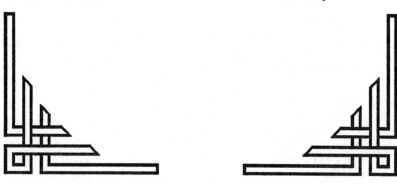

Scripture says:

We hanged our harps upon the willows in the midst thereof.

For there they that carried us away captive required of us a song....

Psalm 137:2,3

You want to come out of your captivity? You've got to get a song. What is so unique here is the ones who held them in captivity knew their avenue of deliverance! The people who held them captive knew how they could come out of it. When they hung their harps on the willows, their captives said, **Sing us one of the songs of Zion** (v. 3).

There are angels in Mount Zion. God fights for Mount Zion. The Lord has strong feelings for Zion! The enemy had the nerve to say, "Sing one of them songs of Zion." Instead of the people saying, "Oh, okay, because we know what it means," they said, **How shall we sing the Lord's song in a strange land?** (v. 4).

The enemy has been speaking to me, "How can you sing a song when you know you need a miracle? How can you sing a song when you know there needs to be a door open? How can you sing a song when you want God to do something for your family? You don't even feel like singing, do you?"

Or the devil will try to keep you out of church and out of corporate praise. "You really should stay home and put your harp up, because they don't know what you've been through. I would just stay at home, it's no use. They will be praising God, and you know you don't feel like praising God. Just stay at home. They are going to be up in your face and you don't feel like being bothered."

Some people play right along with the enemy: "I can't sing a song in a strange land. If God opens the doors for me, then I'll praise Him. If He heals my family, then I'll praise Him. If He gives me the job I asked Him about, then I'll praise Him. If He allows me to get a raise, then I'll praise Him. If my children get saved, then I'll praise Him."

You may be by the rivers of Babylon, but come on out of that strange land and start lifting your voice up in praise and sing unto the Lord. Put the enemy under your feet with a praise break!

How can we sing the Lord's song in a strange land? I'll tell you: "God, I love You. I praise You. I adore You. You are still God! I will bless Your name forever! I will magnify Your name. There is none like You. You are an awesome God. Oh, magnify the Lord with me and let us exalt His name together. You are worthy of all praise.

"You are our hope, our joy, our peace. You are our Waymaker! I will bless You at all times. Your praise shall continually be in my mouth. I will rise and give You praise. At midnight, I'll bless Your name. Seven days a week I'll give glory to You, Lord. At all times I will praise You, because You are worthy of praise and honor and power. Holy are You, O mighty God. Great are You!"

I don't understand how I'm going to come through, but my hope is built on nothing less, than Jesus' blood and righteousness. I trust the sweetest name, and I'm going to give God glory. I'm going to give God praise. It's time to take a praise break! Then walk out of your shackles and bondages, in Jesus' name

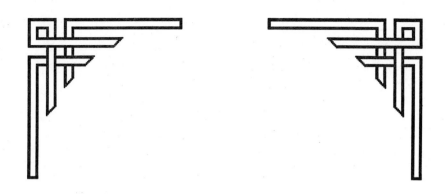

Praise the Lord! Sing to the Lord a new song, praise Him in the assembly of His saints! (Psalm 149:1 AMP).

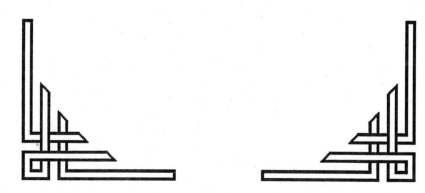

7

Reversed Captivity and Restored Fortunes

Out of the mouth of babes and infants, God has established praise (Psalm 8:2). *Established* or *ordained* means appointed or set aside for a specific purpose.

So the praise that comes out of our mouth is not just a Charismatic feeling. It is not just a Pentecostal feel-me-good. The praise and the celebration of Jesus is not something to keep our church from feeling and looking dead. Praise has been set up by God, not by an individual. If you want to think we're crazy for praising the Lord, then you take it up with Him — the One Who ordained it.

There is a specific purpose why God, all through His Word, keeps challenging us with, **Praise ye the Lord.** So what is the purpose that we've been challenged to put praise in our mouth and let it come from between our lips? I was brought up in the church and told, "If you don't feel like singing, you don't have to sing." I was brought up in the church where the reverend got up and said, "The Lord is in His holy temple. Let all the earth keep silent." And I mean, it was silent for an hour! Then we were dismissed.

God ordained praise to **still the enemy and the avenger** (Psalm 8:2). God has ordained or set aside praise for a specific purpose, because He knows that we have enemies. Not just one big devil, but enemies! He wants to make sure that we don't have to get so physically involved and run our blood pressure up or let things come out of our mouths that shouldn't.

God realized that we would have enemies, so He has set up praise as an offensive weapon for believers. Your enemies will never come to a stop if you don't learn how to praise God. He has ordained praise to come out of *your mouth,* **that thou mightest still the enemy and the avenger** (Psalm 8:2). The word *still* means silence, cause the enemy's power to fail, put down the enemy, to take away his power. God causes the enemy to suffer lack. Praise will take back what the enemy has stolen from you. Praise from your lips weakens the enemy and takes away his power.

Joel 3:1 AMP says, **For behold, in those days, and at that time when I shall reverse the captivity and restore the fortunes of Judah and Jerusalem.** Joel is prophesying that God is getting ready to change some things for us.

God is going to reverse our captivity. Family members are going to be delivered. The wealth of the wicked is going to be loosed into our hands. I'm going to praise God every time I get a chance. I've had some money held up. I'm walking according to the will and the plan of God, and He said the wealth of the wicked is being laid up for the righteous (Proverbs 13:22). I'm walking in righteousness, so I am looking for some megabucks. I'm looking for the desires of my heart to come forth. God said He's going to reverse our captivity and restore our fortunes.

> **I shall...restore the fortunes of Judah** [the praisers] **and Jerusalem** [the Church].
>
> **Joel 3:1** AMP

The Church will never be rich until the people inside the Church are rich, not only financially, but spiritually. Here is the key verse:

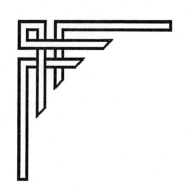

Let the high praises
of God
be in their throats
and a two-edged
sword in their hands
(Psalm 149:6 AMP).

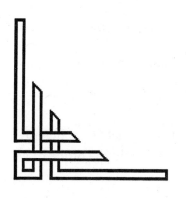

> **I will gather all nations and will bring them down into the Valley of Jehoshaphat....**
>
> **Joel 3:2** AMP

How, when and where will this restoration and reverse of captivity take place? He said, "I will gather all nations." That means every demon force and all of those big giants.

I will gather all nations and will bring them down into the Valley of Jehoshaphat... (Joel 3:2 AMP). You can't hardly see the sun in the valley. Sometimes you can't see to the right or to the left in the valley. You won't even get out of one trial before the next thing comes along and then the next. You will find that every place you turn you're in a battle.

> **I will gather all nations and will bring them down into the Valley of Jehoshaphat, and there will I deal with and execute judgment upon them for [their treatment of] My people and of My heritage Israel, whom they have scattered among the nations and [because] they have divided My land.**
>
> **Joel 3:2** AMP

Some of us are in crisis in our homes, on our jobs, with our families, with our marriages and with our future. We are scattered in many areas of our lives. God is going to reverse and restore, but He's going to only do it in the valley of Jehoshaphat. Let's find out what the valley of Jehoshaphat refers to.

In 2 Chronicles 20, Jehoshaphat was king of the tribe of Judah — the top man of the praisers. When the children of Moab, Ammon and the Ammonites came against Jehoshaphat and the children of Judah, as he began to seek the Lord, God put a word in the mouth of Jahaziel.

Now, Jahaziel wasn't an ordained preacher, a licensed priest, or a national evangelist. He did not hold the office of an apostle or a prophet. He was the temple musician. The Spirit of the Lord came upon the musician in the house. So you don't have to hold any office for God to use you and speak through you.

The Spirit of the Lord came upon Jahaziel and he began to give God's directions. God did not use the king to give direction, but the king responded. Jahaziel told the tribe of Judah, **Be not afraid nor dismayed by reason of this great multitude; for the battle is not yours, but God's** (2 Chronicles 20:15).

Regardless of what you're going through, what the report has been, the battle, where you are now, what you are battling with in your natural life, or your habits, *the battle is not yours, but God's*. God must be up to something. He said, "I'm getting ready to reverse your captivity. I'm getting ready to restore your fortunes." He can only do it when we meet Him in the valley of Jehoshaphat.

So you're crying the blues. I could have cried the blues, took the pity-party route, and said, "Forget ministry." But the more the enemy came against me, the more I preached. God had to get me in a position so the multitudes could come against me so I could meet Him in the valley of Jehoshaphat.

"God, I don't understand why this is happening to me." "Be quiet, I'm giving you a solution." "Once I got my head up above the water, the water came back up again. My mama always had this problem. It's in my family. I've been to church faithfully on time for four Sundays. It looks like by now God should have moved. I've been praying for my husband for fifteen years, and you know, Mary just got saved yesterday and her husband got saved this morning. I just don't understand God. I just feel like giving up " That sounds like some of us.

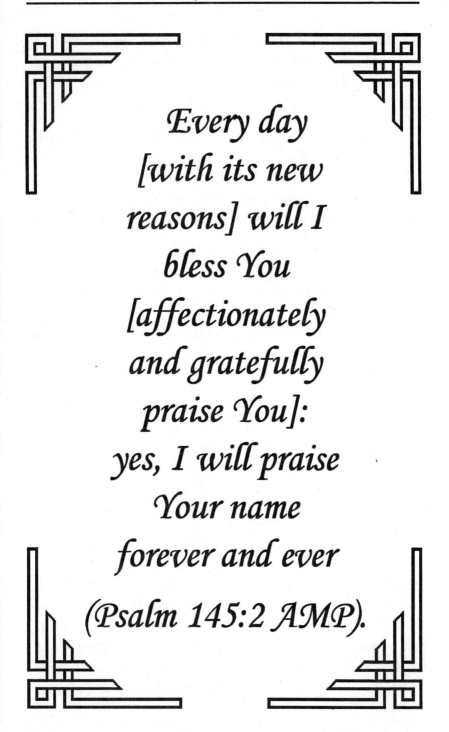

*Every day
[with its new
reasons] will I
bless You
[affectionately
and gratefully
praise You]:
yes, I will praise
Your name
forever and ever
(Psalm 145:2 AMP).*

"Well, God hasn't moved me. He's blessing everybody else all around me with jobs. I've put my application in several places and it looks like nothing is happening. I'm trying to hold on. When I was in the streets, I had a couple thousand dollars in my pocket. But since I've come to church, I mean, I used to drive the best car. I had money every day. But the minute I tried to live right, all hell broke loose. I haven't had $10 since I've been saved." Sounds like some of us!

"I just don't understand. I'm going to Bible study one more time, and I've had seven prophets give me a word. None of their words have manifested. There's nothing to those prophets." Oh, yes, it's just that your season hasn't come yet.

"I've been trying to live right. I haven't seen my sugar daddy since day before yesterday. If I don't get this bill paid by the weekend.... God, if You don't move right now, I've still got his number. See, God helps those who help themselves!"

"I just got laid off from my job, and I was paying my tithe. Just when I was at the brink of getting ahead, I got laid off. I don't understand God."

What you need to know is, God is getting you to the valley of Jehoshaphat, where the multitudes have gathered, and He is still saying, *the battle is not yours, it's the Lord's.*

To morrow go ye down against them... (2 Chronicles 20:16). That means, face your situation. Don't stay at home with the covers pulled up over your head. Face your enemies. The Lord said to go *to them*, so I'm going to go to the valley of Jehoshaphat

> **Ye shall not need to fight in this battle: set yourselves, stand ye still, and see the salvation of the Lord with you, O Judah and Jerusalem: fear not, nor be dismayed; to morrow go out against them: for the Lord will be with you.**
>
> **2 Chronicles 20:17**

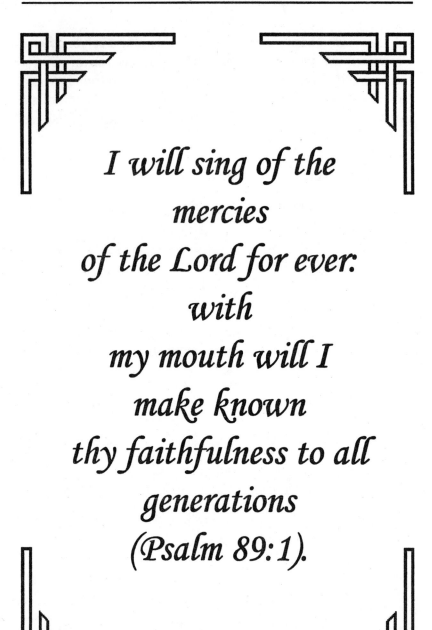

I will sing of the mercies of the Lord for ever: with my mouth will I make known thy faithfulness to all generations (Psalm 89:1).

Go out against them means you've got to put forth some action when you're in the valley of Jehoshaphat. Verse 18 describes Jehoshaphat's action:

> **And Jehoshaphat bowed his head with his face to the ground: and all Judah and the inhabitants of Jerusalem fell before the Lord,** *worshipping the Lord.*

Verse 21 says:

> **And when he [Jehoshaphat] had consulted with the people, he appointed singers unto the Lord, and that should praise the beauty of holiness, as they went out before the army, and to say, Praise the Lord; for his mercy endureth for ever.**

Jehoshaphat *appointed singers.* That means he imposed a law, an obligation, an awesome responsibility upon the singers.

A praise team or a choir is to be *appointed,* it's not to be people who voluntarily come together. Singers in the Bible were warriors. When you join a choir or a musical group, you are putting yourself out on the front line for attack.

Can you imagine a multitude of nations were coming against the children of Judah to destroy them and Jehoshaphat put singers out front?

Jehoshaphat got to the place where he said, "If anything goes down in the tribe of Judah, it will be the singers." Now, God can't keep saying, "Sing unto Me a new song," and all the singers get killed. Jehoshaphat sent out the singers before the army and he told them to sing praises unto the Lord.

You may need to go home, close the door, and go before your enemies with praise in your mouth.

I don't care what the report has been about my children. I'm going to praise God, because the Lord is good and His mercies endure forever! I will praise the Lord. It's a good thing to give thanks unto the Lord. Scripture says that *in* everything give thanks, for this is the will of God in Christ Jesus concerning us, so I am thanking Him for the good He is working in my children, in Jesus' name.

If your mate said he or she isn't coming back, it's a good time to take a praise break! "I don't understand how I am going to get through all next week." It's a good time to take a praise break! "My car broke down, and I don't have the finances to fix it right now." Take a praise break!

Jehoshaphat appointed singers and told them to go out and start praising the Lord before the enemy, and as they began to sing, "God, I love You. I praise You. Hallelujah to the Lamb. This is the day You have made. I will rejoice and be glad in it," the enemy became confused.

God said, "I want to reverse your captivity. I want to reverse the spirit of oppression that has afflicted you. I want to reverse your lack of strength. I want to reverse your words, 'Nobody loves me.' I want to reverse it so praise can come out of your mouth and change your circumstances and you can get back what the enemy has stolen."

How do we praise? Tell God how much you love Him. Tell Him He is great and there is none like Him. Put praise in your mouth, and He will shut your enemy up.

When the praisers completed their task in 2 Chronicles 20, all that was left to do was to collect the spoils of battle — riches and precious jewels (v. 25).

I'm ready to gather the spoils of the enemy. If you aren't, then I'll see you later. You'll still be on pity-party street, your address is the house of depression, and your name is worrywart. And you came to the blues brothers. Or, you can take this word and say, "God, You set me up because You are reversing some things in my life."

Praise ye the Lord.
Blessed
is the man that
feareth the
Lord, that delighteth
greatly
in his commandments
(Psalm112:1).

Now, let's go to Malachi, chapter 3, verse 4:

Then shall the offering of Judah and Jerusalem be pleasant unto the Lord, as in the days of old, and as in former years.

As I mentioned earlier, the word *Judah* means praise and the word *Jerusalem* is always symbolic of the local church. So the word of the Lord is saying, "All that comes forth out of a praiser in the local house shall be satisfying unto the Lord.

Joel 3:18 says, **And it shall come to pass in that day** [when the church absolutely becomes the praising church], **that the mountains shall drop down new wine....** [*New wine* is a type of the flow of the Holy Spirit.] **And the hills shall flow with milk** [or nourishment], **and all the rivers of Judah shall flow with waters, and a fountain shall come forth of the house of the Lord, and shall water** [or bring back alive] **the valley of Shittim** [which represents dead, dried up, ritualistic religious order].

The Holy Spirit is springing up in us in this hour like never before. We don't have to plead with God. We don't have to beg God, but there is a new move of the Holy Spirit, and out of the rivers of Judah come the praises of God. Notice, it didn't say that it comes out of only one river. We'll come into an order where even the pastor or the leader is not the center of attention — God Himself is the main attraction. Out of the bellies of the praisers will flow life-changing words to water our religious orders.

Many people believe church is a drag. They attend but say they're getting nothing out of it. But there's a change of order that is coming and it's not believing in a certain denomination or in a certain tradition. There's an excitement that's coming from the believers. The rivers of the Spirit are flowing and the fountain of God is being stirred up.

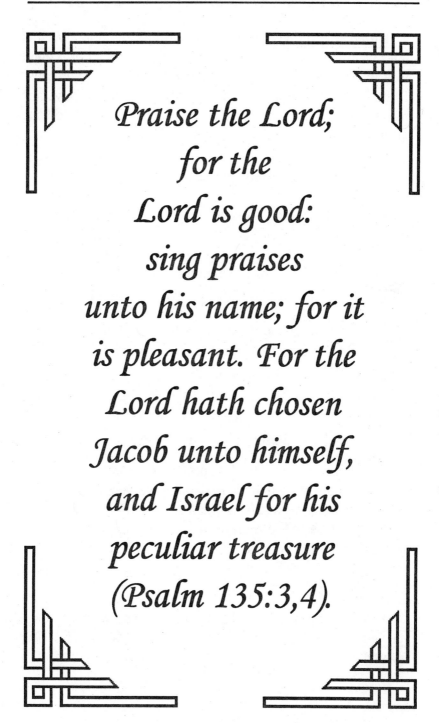

*Praise the Lord;
for the
Lord is good:
sing praises
unto his name; for it
is pleasant. For the
Lord hath chosen
Jacob unto himself,
and Israel for his
peculiar treasure
(Psalm 135:3,4).*

I used to sing, "Give me that old-time religion." Well, I don't want that because some of the stuff I came out of, I don't want to go back to. I don't want the old-time religion, because if I go back to it, I couldn't wear earrings, I wouldn't have any makeup on, and I wouldn't be in the pulpit. I'm going to hang out in Judah!

Prophetic Destiny for Judah: Victory!

In Genesis 29, Judah was born to Leah who had been given to Jacob as a wife rather than Rachel. It's a bad thing to get married and have your husband reject you. When you are rejected from the very beginning, that must be pretty bad. Can you imagine when Jacob thought he had Rachel and he woke up the next morning and it was Leah. But I don't want to zero in on that. Judah was the fourth son born to Leah, but even having children for Jacob didn't change his love for her.

Instead of trying to please Jacob, Leah turned her attention to pleasing God. God was so honored with Leah naming her fourth son Judah that his lineage will always be blessed until Jesus comes back. Scripture tells us that Jesus came from the line of Judah.

If we would bring it down to our day, we need Jesus to come on the scene. Hebrews tells us that Jesus springs up out of Judah [our praise]. Instead of murmuring, complaining and trying to fix it, we need to learn how to open our mouths and give God glory, then Jesus will come on the scene, because He comes forth out of Judah [our praise].

Scripture reveals that Judah wasn't always pleasing to God, yet because Judah represented "praise to the Lord," God favored her.

In Genesis, chapter 49, when Jacob called his sons to his

bedside to prophesy to them before his death, he said of Judah, **Judah, thou art he whom thy brethren shall praise** (v. 8). If you become a praiser, I don't care who rejects you or dislikes you, the prophetic word for a praiser is that *your brethren shall admire you.*

They may talk about you at first, but they will keep hanging around until they realize something is different. Their attitude and disposition will change, because there's a word out that God will bring to pass: "Your brethren shall praise you."

Jacob also prophesied of Judah, **Thy hand shall be in the neck of thine enemies** (Genesis 49:8). In other words, "Every time you open your mouth and praise God, you're getting ready to choke the devil." When you get a good choke on somebody, they can't do too much harm. That's why the devil dislikes praisers, and that's why the enemy tried to stop praise in the church. As long as he can just have a religious order, it is no threat to the devil. But when the Church rises up to be praisers, he knows that he just as well take a hike! His major work is done there.

Not only shall his hand be upon the neck of his enemies and he become victorious, but **...thy father's children shall bow down before thee** (Genesis 49:8). That means those who are around you are going to have to step back and express approval, then they're going to have to agree with you and come and see what's going on in your life.

Verse 9 says, **Judah is a lion's whelp.** That means you are a baby cub. A lion takes care of its cub. You don't have to worry about defending yourself. Your praises make it God's business to take care of you and to protect you. So Judah is a lion's whelp. Who would have the nerve to pick on a lion's cub, because when you mess with a cub, you stir up the old lion.

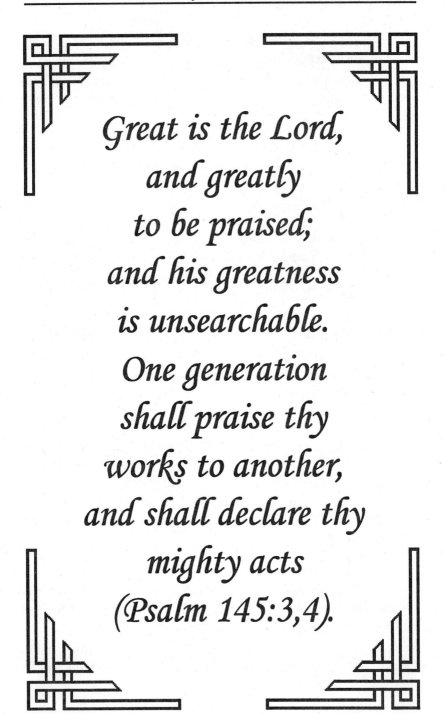

Great is the Lord,
and greatly
to be praised;
and his greatness
is unsearchable.
One generation
shall praise thy
works to another,
and shall declare thy
mighty acts
(Psalm 145:3,4).

I love watching jungle movies that show the animal kingdom. When you see the baby cubs playing, you never see the lion standing with the cubs. They are always hidden in some kind of bush not too far back, crouching down and relaxing. And as long as the babies are playing, the old lion remains at rest. But the minute the sound of that baby cub's voice changes, the old lion rises up to see who's messing with her babies.

You know, there is a difference when we praise God when everything is going all right, and when we praise God when we still can't understand what is going on and things are going bad and crushing in on us. There's a joyous sound when everything is going well, and then there's a different sound when we praise God in spite of our circumstances.

Every time the sound of your praise changes, the old lion - the Lion of the tribe of Judah, Jesus Christ — rises up to see what's going on. That's why we are a dangerous people when someone messes with us! When the enemy messes with us, he arouses the Lion of the tribe of Judah!

Jacob also prophesied over Judah, **The sceptre** [the authority and power] **shall not depart from Judah** (Genesis 49:10). Your praise to God has power and authority in it. It's not just an empty hallelujah and a thank-You, Jesus, but every time you put praise in your mouth, it has rulership with God. That means it gets His attention.

Verse 10 goes on, **...nor a lawgiver from between his feet, until Shiloh** [Jesus] **come; and unto him shall the gathering of the people be.**

Deuteronomy 33:7 contains Moses' blessing of Judah before his death:

Hear, Lord, the voice of Judah, and bring him unto his people: let his hands be sufficient for him; and be thou an help to him from his enemies.

If you are a praiser, you are blessed, not in doing your own thing in praising, but in following God's principles for praising Him.

If you're planning on going to heaven, you'd better get used to a loud voice of praise. If you have accepted Jesus as your Lord and Savior, then you're going to heaven.

Now, I haven't found this in the Bible, but this is Pat McKinstry's interpretation. I believe some of the people who have never gotten into praise, when they get to heaven, they will go into a classroom to learn how to praise the Lamb Who is ever being praised.

Every time you open your mouth in praise, God stands at attention, because He hears a sound of Judah.

We're so different than the angels because our will is involved. We "will" or "choose" to praise Him. Anytime you make up your mind to praise Him and every time He hears a hallelujah, He stands at attention and gives you His full attention.

Praise brings people into unity, and when God hears you, He inhabits or comes where you are (Psalm 22:3). And not only does He give you His attention and come where you are to inhabit your praise, His hands become sufficient for you. Your praise gets your needs out of God's hand. We used to sing, "He's got the whole world in His hands." Your praise picks out of God's hand. That's why we don't ever have to worry about coming to God and saying, "Gimme, gimme, gimme." He just says, "Come into My face and once you get in My face, you'll get My hand."

*Let everything that
has breath
and every breath of
life praise the Lord!
(Psalm 150:6 AMP).*

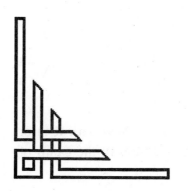

So every time I praise God, my praises take care of my needs. You can't just praise God and tell Him how great He is, how wonderful He is and how awesome He is without God doing something for you.

When a woman tells her man, "You've got such broad shoulders," he stands tall and proud. And when someone tells a woman, "I love you in that color, pink is your color," she fills her closet with the whole family of pink!

If praise in the natural does something to us, how much more do you think the Lamb is affected when we tell Him, "I love You. You're the best thing that ever happened to me"? God wants to do something for you when you praise Him. He will become a help to you from your enemies. Your praise fights for you, so don't mess with a praiser!

God is not only a shepherd, a provider and a healer, but He is a warrior. When we praise Him, we stir up the war in Him. He becomes a help for us from our enemies. I tell people, "He's almost like a windshield." You know how you are speeding down the highway, especially at night, and bugs splatter all over your window? When I saw that one night, I said, "That's how my praise is. The enemy was getting ready to throw something at me, but as I praised God, He put up a windshield [a hedge]. The enemy can't get to me! Praising God builds up a hedge for us, and He becomes a protector for us.

In Numbers 2:3, the Lord was telling Moses how to set up the tribes around the tabernacle. And when he dealt with Judah he said, **And on the east side toward the rising of the sun shall they of the standard of the camp of Judah pitch throughout their armies....**

When you become a praiser, no matter how dark it is or what's going on in your life, if you hang out in the camp of

Judah, instead of murmuring and complaining, after awhile the sun is going to shine. The praiser is the first one to see daybreak and see the sun shining. Then verse 5 says to tell Judah to pitch their tent next to the tribe of Issachar and verse 7 says next to the tribe of Zebulun. These were the three tribes that hung out together, sitting around the tabernacle.

Issachar means reward and *Zebulun* means habitation. The Lord told Moses to tell Judah, "You'll be the first not only to see the sun rise, but you're going to be the first to recognize the Son when you become a praiser."

There is a reward for being a praiser, because you'll hang out with Issachar. And not only is there a reward for being a praiser, but you're with the tribe of Zebulun, which means that rewards hang out with you. You are hanging out in expectancy of harvest.

Overcoming a Canaanite Spirit

You can't be a praiser and stay defeated. You can't be a praiser and have poverty, sickness and sorrow in your house, because a praiser causes sadness to flee, mourning to be done away with.

In Judges, chapter 1, the children of Judah didn't know what to do after the death of Joshua. They had to go up against the Canaanites. (The Canaanites always fought against God's people.) The Canaanite spirit is the spirit that keeps you from becoming what God has called you to be. The Canaanite spirit means to be pressed and trampled down so you can never rise to your purpose and call. And the Canaanite spirit always went up against the tribe of Israel and loved fighting Judah. It fought against the tribe of Judah more than any of the other tribes

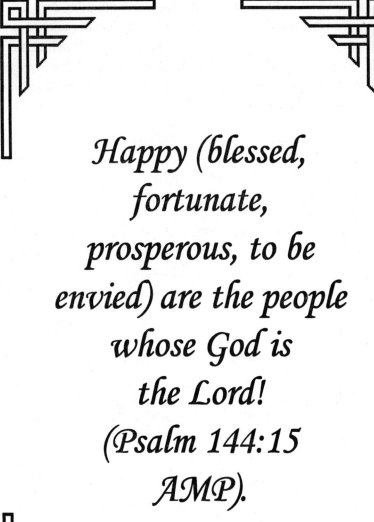

Happy (blessed, fortunate, prosperous, to be envied) are the people whose God is the Lord! (Psalm 144:15 AMP).

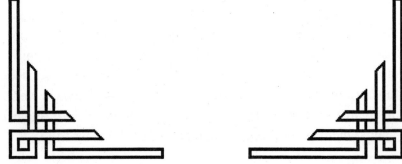

If it can keep you thinking that God can't change things for you, you will never praise God. You've got to get to the place where you believe God's Word in spite of what is going on — the circumstances or the adversity. Judah believed God's Word and they sang His praise.

Just because you become a believer doesn't mean you are devil-proof. You're not exempt from the devil messing with you. But you've got to get to the place where you know in whom you believe. Then your circumstances will not dictate your praise. Your problems and storms will not regulate your praise. You will praise God regardless because He is worthy to be praised.

The Canaanites tried to keep Judah out of the promised land. The Lord said, **Judah shall go up: behold, I have delivered the land into his hand** (Judges 1:2).

God has already given us some promises about our seed, our finances and our joy.

Joshua was dead, so who was going to fight against the Canaanites? The Lord sent Judah out first and Judah turned around and said, "Can I take Simeon?" Some people say Simeon means hearing by faith, but if you read the story of Simeon, he was a type that anytime you pray, you will hear from God

The Lord said, "Go on and take Simeon." So Judah said, "Simeon, come up with me into my lot. Then, when it's your time I'll go with you to your lot."

Send Judah Out First

There are some things you've got to *pray* to get and other things you've got to *praise* to get. When we are being pressed down, the Lord says, "Send Judah out first." When things get tough for you, send Judah out first. Don't call your best friend, but send Judah out first. Even if you've got a good lawyer, send Judah out first. "I don't know how I'm going to make it." Send Judah out first. Open your mouth and give God praise and glory. Send Judah out first!

When the devil tries to make you feel bad about your circumstances, or he wants you to have a pity party over your home being messed up, it's time for a praise break. "Hallelujah to the Lamb Who sits upon the throne. He is worthy of all of our praise." Send Judah out first.

There's a raising praise that will cause you to soar above the storms. I have literally flown above storms, looked out of the airplane window and still saw the storm, the lightning, and all of that, but we were in smooth sailing. God can put you in a place that no matter what it is, He can bring you out of it and through it.

Remember when the Prophet Isaiah told Hezekiah to get his house in order because he was going to die? (Isaiah 38:1). Most of us don't want to hear a word like that. We would rather hear, "Go home and on the back porch, raise up the mat and you'll find $5,000, saith the Lord." You wouldn't even have time to fall out and the ushers catch you. You would make a beeline for your house!

You may wake up to a phone call and be told one of your children just got in trouble. You may go back to the doctor and get a bad report. You may wake up to a phone call that says, "I'm not coming home to live with you anymore." You may wake up to a phone call that says your job has been cut because of downsizing.

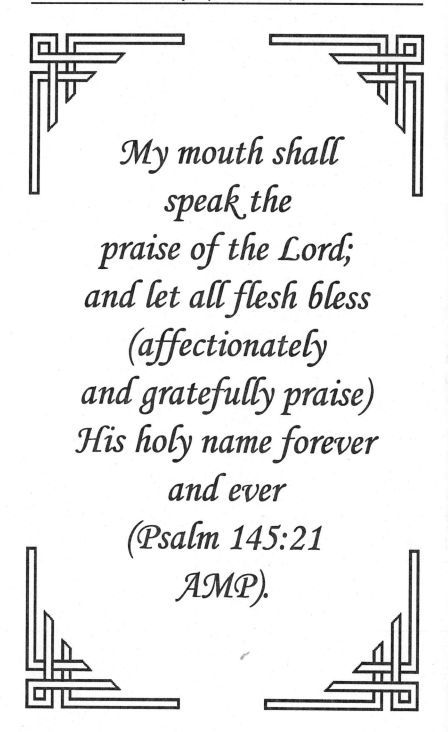

My mouth shall speak the praise of the Lord; and let all flesh bless (affectionately and gratefully praise) His holy name forever and ever (Psalm 145:21 AMP).

When the Prophet Isaiah left, **Hezekiah turned his face toward the wall, and prayed unto the Lord** (Isaiah 38:2). We stop there and think Hezekiah only prayed. But when you read further in this chapter, Hezekiah got through praying and he told God'

> **For the grave cannot praise thee, death can *not* celebrate thee: they that go down into the pit cannot hope for thy truth.**
>
> **Isaiah 38:18**

Hezekiah knew what would get to God because he had a heart of worship. God seeks those who will worship Him in spirit and in truth. Hezekiah knew that God would inhabit his praises. He also knew that God pays attention to praisers. A praiser moves God and changes His mind.

Verses 4 and 5 of Isaiah, chapter 38, say:

> **Then came the word of the Lord to Isaiah, saying,**
>
> **Go, and say to Hezekiah, Thus saith the Lord, the God of David thy father, I have heard thy prayer, and I have seen thy tears: behold, I will add unto thy days fifteen years.**

Zion is calling us to a higher place of praise. Hallelujah!

I don't know what you're facing. Maybe everything is all right with you. But just in case the devil has a trick or a trap waiting on you, I'm going to give God a hallelujah. When the devil comes against you, remember, *no weapon formed against you shall prosper*! Hallelujah!

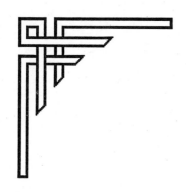

*Seven times a day do
I praise thee because
of thy righteous
judgments
(Psalm 119:164).*

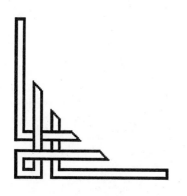

8

The Power of Corporate Worship

And it came to pass, when Joshua had spoken unto the people, that the seven priests bearing the seven trumpets of rams' horns passed on before the Lord, and blew with the trumpets: and the ark of the covenant of the Lord followed them.

And the armed men [the intercessors] went before the priests that blew with the trumpets, and the rereward came after the ark, the priests going on, and blowing with the trumpets.

Joshua 6:8,9

In our church, there is not one service held without starting with half an hour of intercession, because we want to send the armed men out before we, the priests, get there. The musicians, ushers, those receiving the offering, and those reading the Scripture — everyone who is involved in the worship service — must be there half an hour before worship for intercession. If you miss it and you are the main organist, you won't play for that service. We are getting you ready to lead the people into worship, and the Lord is bringing the body into no strange worship.

The intercessors went before the priests that blew with the trumpets, and the rerewards came after the ark. Something happens once the presence of the Lord comes into a place. *Rereward* means to gather in order to destroy or consume

111

When we as a people begin to worship collectively and the presence of the Lord gets in the house, it gathers in order to destroy.

When the presence of the Lord gets into the house, we don't have to take time to exorcise devils. The presence of the Lord will destroy and consume or drive them out. The Word says, "This comes in after the ark." It will save us a whole lot of time if we just usher in the rereward of the Lord.

Verse 13 again says you have the intercessors, the priests, the presence of the Lord and the rereward — the consuming force that is released in the presence of the Lord. This is why when we, as a body, begin to learn what it is to worship the Lord, we won't have to worry about pumping and priming and telling the people, "Come on." After the blowing of the trumpets and the intercession, God's presence fills the house.

Let's look at a few of the things that happen in corporate worship. The first thing is music. God commanded the making of the instruments. And if you read about David, he was one of the musicians who made over 4,000 instruments. He made them, not for Michael Jackson's group, but for those of us who will worship and praise the Lord today.

It is very important that we, as leaders, stop hiring musicians and begin to *appoint* musicians and singers in the house who are worshippers. We must stop letting just anyone join the choir or sing in the praise team. The leaders must recognize those who have a heart after God.

In my church, the organist's position was vacant for three years. I had many friends say they wanted to play. But I laid across that bench and said, "Lord, You send someone in who is first of all after Your heart. Second, they must have the vision of this church "

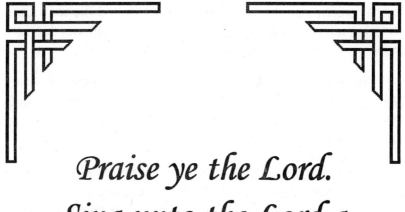

Praise ye the Lord.
Sing unto the Lord a
new song, and his
praise
in the congregation
of saints
(Psalm 149:1).

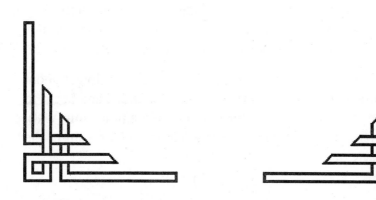

There was power when the trumpeters and the musicians became as one, so music has a lot to do with our worship service.

Isaiah 42:10 speaks of singing a new song unto the Lord. Every Spirit-filled believer can sing a new song unto the Lord. When we become praisers individually, it won't be a job to praise corporately.

God is bringing the church into knowledge where a lot of our songs need to be kicked out. It's time now for climbing up the rough side of the mountain, speaking to the challenges to be removed. I tell our singers and our choir to make sure the songs are talking directly to God or saying something about God, but to stop singing about our troubles! We need to make sure the songs are in line with God's Word.

Isaiah 52:8 says, **Thy watchmen shall lift up the voice....** If the leaders aren't worshippers, you can forget about the body being worshippers. I tell the people at my church, "If I get to the place where I'm missing it, find a church that will keep you before the Lord and feed you with His Word." It's time we quit staying in a church just because we were born into it, our grandmother helped build it, or where the watchmen can't even lift their voice and sing.

When we begin to sing unto the Lord together — the watchmen (intercessors) and the congregation — it brings unity. **Thy watchmen shall lift up the voice; with the voice together shall they sing: for they shall see eye to eye...** (Isaiah 52:8).

When they begin to sing unto the Lord, they forget about their problems, or about how they were offended and begin to see **eye to eye, when the Lord shall bring again Zion** (v. 8). Twenty-four hours a day there was praise and worship in the tabernacle of God.

When we begin to sing together, guess what happens? The waste places of Jerusalem are built up

Break forth into joy, sing together, ye waste places of Jerusalem: for the Lord hath comforted his people, he hath redeemed Jerusalem.

Isaiah 52:9

"The waste places of Jerusalem" mean everyone in the local church will become fruitful. Then God will comfort His people, bring back His glory and redeem Jerusalem. God's glory is returning to the local church because we are beginning to sing new songs unto Him and seeing eye to eye.

Lifting Up Your Hands

Then we have the lifting of the hands in worship. It's time that we realize when we do certain things in the house of God, it's not just because we are Pentecostal. I lifted my hands for years and didn't know the power there was in lifting my hands. I just thought because I was raised in a holiness church, that's what they did.

Today, out of adoration of the Lord, there are times when I'm driving that I hold onto the steering wheel with one hand and wave the other in worship to the Lord. People think I'm waving at them, but I'm waving at God! It's an act of blessing God, as we read in Psalm 134:

Behold, bless ye the Lord, all ye servants of the Lord, which by night stand in the house of the Lord.

Lift up your hands in the sanctuary, and bless the Lord.

Verses 1,2

Every time I lift my hands, I don't even have to add my mouth to it. But every time I am in the sanctuary and I lift my hands, I tell God, "You are worthy. There's none like You. You are the holy God of Israel. O blessed Redeemer!"

Psalm 141:2 says the lifting of the hands is **as the evening sacrifice.** Lamentations 2:19 says, **...lift up thy hands toward him for the life of thy young children....** You may have children you want God to deliver. You can say, "Lord, I heard I could lift my hands up for my young children, and You will bring deliverance."

Psalm 143:6 says, **I stretch forth my hands unto thee: my soul thirsteth after thee, as a thirsty land.** With uplifted hands you are saying, "My mind, will and emotions are thirsty for You, Lord." Every time we lift our hands, we are saying, "Lord, more than anything, I want You."

When a child wants up, they lift their hands and if they can talk, they say, "Pick me up." As we lift our hands in corporate worship, we can say, "Lord, pick me up."

Exodus 17:11 says that as long as Moses held up his hand, Israel prevailed. There is power in the lifting of our hands because our hands speak. Our hands also speak for surrender. You can go all over the world and not speak the people's language, but if someone puts a gun in your back, you automatically lift your hands in surrender.

The Clapping of Hands

The clapping of our hands is another form of worship and an expression of victory. Job 27:23 says, **Men shall clap their hands at him, and shall hiss him out of his place.** I found out that clapping of the hands tells the devil, "Back out of here."

*Exalt ye the Lord
our God,
and worship at his
footstool; for
he is holy
(Psalm 99:5).*

We used to have clapping services where the saints just put their hands together. Every time we put our hands together and clapped, we were telling the devil, "Back out of here."

Something happened in Lamentations 2:15 when the enemy of the Israelites captured them and put them in a circle:

> **All that pass by clap their hands at thee; they hiss and wag their head at the daughter of Jerusalem, saying, Is this the city that men call The perfection of beauty, The joy of the whole earth?**

The devil used clapping as a gesture against us. Ezekiel 25:6,7 says:

> **For thus saith the Lord God; Because thou hast clapped thine hands, and stamped with the feet, and rejoiced in heart with all thy despite against the land of Israel;**
>
> **Behold, therefore I will stretch out mine hand upon thee, and will deliver thee for a spoil to the heathen; and I will cut thee off from the people, and I will cause thee to perish out of the countries: I will destroy thee; and thou shalt know that I am the Lord.**

Every time we go to church, we shouldn't have to tell people, "Put your hands together and praise God." We should get in our minds, God is using clapping — what the devil used to use to make fun of our captivity. The Lord has turned this thing around, and we are telling the devil, "You don't have me."

Standing

Standing was an expression of victory. There was never a time in the presence of God when anyone sat down. I believe there's a time that we can sit and there's a time that we should stand in the presence of the Lord. Standing is an acknowledgement of His authority and reign.

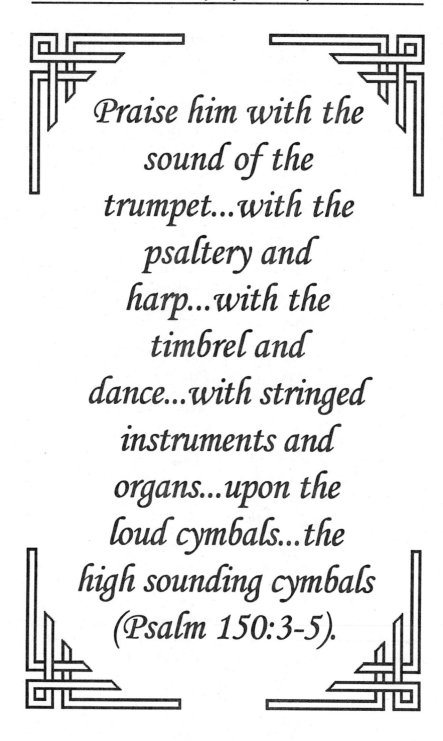

Praise him with the sound of the trumpet...with the psaltery and harp...with the timbrel and dance...with stringed instruments and organs...upon the loud cymbals...the high sounding cymbals (Psalm 150:3-5).

When a judge walks into a courtroom, everybody stands. If Queen Elizabeth was to walk in a room, everyone would stand, or they would be fined for remaining in their seat. It is a recognition of her authority.

Why is it that it is so difficult to stand in the house of the Lord during the time that we are worshipping and giving adoration to God, acknowledging His control, His reign, and His rule?

Bowing

Bowing is another form of worship. In Matthew 2:11 when the wise men saw Jesus, they **fell down, and worshipped him.** The wise men recognized who Jesus was as a young child, so they bowed before Him.

When we bow before the Lord, we are expressing, "Lord, You are Lord of lords and King of kings."

Psalm 72:9 says, **They that dwell in the wilderness shall bow before him; and his enemies shall lick the dust.**

Perhaps you are saying right now, "I'm in a wilderness experience. It's a dry time, a hard time, a difficult time. I can't see my way out. I don't know which way I'm going. I'm walking by faith. Famine and storms are blowing in my life."

The Lord says, "Instead of falling down and complaining and murmuring, learn how to worship Me. While you are worshipping Me, your enemies will lick the dust!"

Instead of saying, "Satan, I bind you. Come out of here. Give up," bow down in worship to the Lord The best time to worship is when you are in the wilderness

Dancing Before the Lord

Another form of worship is *dancing* before the Lord. When we dance before the Lord, we don't have to worry about anyone holding us. When I used to dance, Chubby Checkers was just coming out. He came out with, "Come On, Baby, Let's Do the Twist." And every time I heard that song, I'd do the twist. But every time I danced, no one had to hold me up. Where do we get this stuff that we get real crazy and step on somebody's feet? How in the world can God give you the victory and you just stepped on my feet? You've got the victory, and I'm trying to get delivered of pain!

Dancing before the Lord is symbolic of putting the enemy under your feet as Paul described in Romans 16:20: **And the God of peace shall bruise Satan under your feet shortly.**

Every time you dance, you are telling the devil, "I'm subduing you." Not only are you praising the Lord, but you are saying, "My enemies can no longer triumph over me." Dancing is an act of worship. You don't even need music to dance before the Lord.

If you want to praise the Lord in dance and you're in a tight corner, just say, "Excuse me." The intellect of some people may say, "I'm not dancing, because God is not crazy. The Holy Spirit is not in you for you to act crazy and dance. He's got a much bigger job than to make you happy and to give you a thrill. He comes for you to be an effective witness."

While that is partially true, there is a time of celebration where you get excited and dance before the Lord. It is saying, "God, how I celebrate You!"

You don't need the Holy Spirit to dance before the Lord. If that's the case, then Michael Jackson must have Him and all of His gifts The Father is looking for worshippers. But He wants

His worshippers to have some sense and worship Him according to His pattern and His blueprint so His glory can come in and fill the house. Then He can begin to take over and consume your enemies!

Jeremiah 31:4 says:

Again I will build thee, and thou shalt be built, O virgin of Israel: thou shalt again be adorned with thy tabrets, and shalt go forth in the dances of them that make merry.

Verse 6 says:

For there shall be a day, that the watchmen upon the mount Ephraim shall cry, Arise ye, and let us go up to Zion unto the Lord our God.

It's time to worship the Lord with an understanding that while we are worshipping, things are being done in the spiritual realm.

Before I get to the house of the Lord, I'm going to worship God as an individual. Then, when I get to the local house with my brothers and sisters, we're going to magnify the Lord in corporate worship. We're going to lift our hands in the sanctuary.

Sometimes you have to tell your soul [your mind, will, intellect and emotions], "Bless the Lord, O my soul. I'm not going to be distracted, soul. But with all that is within me, I'm going to bless Your name, Lord God Almighty!"